Victorious

...*In all these things we are more than victorious through Him who loved us.*

Romans 8:37 HCSB

# *Introduction*

*Every woman has a story.*
*Every woman has a struggle.*
*Every woman has a promise of victory.*

Romans 8:37 assures us that God has given us the power in all things to conquer and be victorious. We need not fear life or death, things present or things to come, because God loves us and sent His Son, Jesus, to give us the victory.

This is not a promise with conditions attached: "If you do this, God will do that." Christ has already accomplished it!

- We are free from judgment because Christ died for our sin and we have His righteousness.
- We are free from defeat because Christ lives in us by His Spirit and we share His life.
- We are free from discouragement because Christ is coming for us and we will share His glory.
- We are free from fear because Christ intercedes for us and we cannot be separated from His love.

This study is a tribute to the women in the New Testament, whose lives were touched and forever changed by Jesus. Some of these women you will meet by name, others will be known by their situation. Their very raw and personal stories demonstrate the power of Christ to conquer anything that seeks to come against the victory that is ours in Him. As we dig deep into each woman's encounter with Jesus, our hearts will be radically changed and compelled to follow Him with nothing less than all of our lives.

We make a grievous error when we believe that the women in the Bible are somehow irrelevant to the lives we are living today. Nothing could be further from the truth. Though times may have changed, our struggles have not. The women of the New Testament will quickly become your friends and confidants and you will truly identify with their hearts.

As you come to a deeper knowledge and love for Jesus through the lives of these women, know that He is in the midst of your story and your struggle. He is there to help you walk in the victory that He has already won for you when He died on the cross and rose!

***Remember you are more than victorious in Christ!***

# How to Study

Welcome to "**Victorious II**", a study of New Testament women who walked victoriously with Jesus!

*Here are some suggestions to help you enjoy a daily, rich, satisfying time with God in His Word.*

1. Set aside 35-45 minutes of quiet time each day. It is a good idea to have a basket prepared in advance with your Bible, pens, highlighters and study. Keep your basket in the same place so it is readily available when you awake.

2. Before you begin each day remember to pray. Ask God to open your mind and heart and yield to the teaching of the Holy Spirit.

3. Each New Testament woman's life is divided into three segments for you to study:

   ❖ **Her Story**
   This segment provides an opportunity to gain insight into each woman's life. It is here where you will discover interesting facts about her life and her role in the New Testament.

   ❖ **Her Struggle**
   This segment uses Scripture to identify each woman's unique struggle. The Word of God will help you to personally pinpoint problem areas that you may be experiencing in your own life.

   ❖ **Her Victory**
   This segment reveals how each woman was able to walk victoriously with Jesus! As you dig deep into God's Word, Scripture will teach you how you can apply these truths in your own life so that you too can be victorious.

4. Enjoy many "**SELAH**" moments along the way.

   *Selah* means to "*pause and to calmly think about*". As you come upon a *selah* moment you want to stop to carefully weigh and consider the truth that is being presented. You may want to rush and answer the next question, but take the time to ponder the deep truths that are being presented. These *selah* moments offer great learning opportunities.

*Purpose in your heart to be victorious!*

# Study Lessons

| | | |
|---|---|---|
| Week 1 | Mary, Mother of Jesus | Victorious over Selfishness |
| Week 2 | Elizabeth | Victorious over Discouragement |
| Week 3 | Anna | Victorious over Loneliness |
| Week 4 | The Woman with an Issue of Blood | Victorious over Suffering |
| Week 5 | The Samaritan Woman | Victorious over Idolatry |
| Week 6 | The Woman Caught in Adultery | Victorious over Sexual Sin |
| Week 7 | Mary at Bethany | Victorious over the World |
| Week 8 | Mary Magdalene | Victorious over the Darkness |
| Week 9 | Tabitha | Victorious over Death |

Then Mary said,
"Behold the maidservant of the Lord!
Let it be to me according to your word."
And the angel departed from her.


Luke 1:38

# *Mary, Mother of Jesus*

## Victorious over Selfishness

*Above all the grace and the gifts that Christ gives to His beloved is that of overcoming self.*

Francis of Assisi

**The <u>Me Me Me</u> Generation!**

It is not a surprise that <u>The Me Me Me Generation</u> was the title of a cover story featured on the May 2013 issue of Time Magazine. Writer Joel Stein highlights a current statistic that must not be overlooked:

*The incidence of narcissistic personality disorder is nearly three times as high for people in their 20s as for the generation that's now 65 or older, according to the National Institutes of Health; 58 percent more college students scored higher on a narcissism scale in 2009 than in 1982.*

What is narcissism? It is a term that originated with Narcissus in Greek mythology who fell in love with his own image reflected in a pool of water. Currently it is used to describe a person characterized by egotism, vanity, pride or selfishness. Often categorized as a clinical disorder, the believer in Christ quickly recognizes that this is not a medical problem, but a *sin* issue. John MacArthur makes the following comment:

*Man's basic problem is preoccupation with self. He is innately beset with narcissism, a condition named after the Greek mythological character Narcissus, who spent his life admiring his reflection in a pool of water. In the final analysis, every sin results from preoccupation with self. We sin because we are totally selfish, totally devoted to ourselves, rather than to God and to others.*

In his book, <u>The Shadow of the Cross</u>, Walter Chantry remarks that selfishness is the controlling force of sinful living. He explains that it is this motive which pulsates through the natural mind, emotions and will; **self-pleasing, self-serving, living for self**.

We can rejoice that Jesus came to deliver us from **"SELF"**! His love and sacrifice on our behalf made it possible for us to live no longer for ourselves, but for Him who died for us and rose again.

How fitting it is, that we would learn from the mother of Jesus, how to live a "**selfless**" life. Imagine sharing a time of coffee and fellowship with Mary this week. She is a spiritual mother and the wisdom and example of her life offers us deep insights into living a life beyond ourselves. Be sure to listen carefully and consider every word to ***discover how she became victorious over selfishness.***

# Mary's Story

*Far from presenting Mary with a halo and an angelic stare on her face, Scripture reveals her as an ordinary girl of common means from a peasant's town in a poor region of Israel. If you had met Mary before Jesus was miraculously conceived, you might not have noticed her at all.*

**Read Luke 1:26-38.**

1. *What do we know about Mary?* She was a Jewish girl of the tribe of Judah and a descendant of David. She was engaged to a carpenter named Joseph and both were of humble means. Since Jewish girls married young, it is likely that Mary was a teenager when the angel appeared to her.

    What important fact do we learn about Mary from Luke 1:27?

    ⊷SELAH⊶
    ### Kiddushin
    *This is the Hebrew word for a legal engagement we call a "betrothal" in English. Kiddushin was as legally binding as marriage and usually lasted a full year prior to a wedding. The couple was deemed husband and wife and only a legal divorce could dissolve the marriage contract. During this time the couple lived separately from one another and had no physical relations whatsoever. One of the main reasons for kiddushin was to demonstrate the commitment of both partners to the marriage prior to the wedding.*

2. What values does our culture promote regarding virginity and commitment in marriage?

3. How do these values compare to biblical values? Use Scripture to support your answer.

4. Mary was called to be the woman through whom Christ would come. It was a calling that came with a high cost, because it carried with it the stigma of an unwed pregnancy. Although Mary was a virgin, the world would think otherwise.

    **God's calling on our lives will always come with a high cost. Give some examples.**

5. If you found yourself in Mary's situation, what would your first thoughts be about Joseph?

6. Read Matthew 1:18-21. How did God go before Mary to prepare Joseph's heart?

7. *"Let it be to me according to your word!"* In order to accept God's call for her life, Mary had to lay aside her plans. This would include the concern for her reputation and her desire to be socially acceptable.

   **How difficult is it for you to surrender your plan for your life to accept God's good and perfect will?**

8. How do we learn Mary became pregnant in Luke 1:35?

∾SELAH∾

*The word overshadow means "to cover with a cloud," as in the cloud of Shekinah glory in the Old Testament or the cloud of Transfiguration in the New Testament. This cloud was a visible manifestation of the glory and presence of God; this means that the same power of God that was with Moses and others in the Old Testament was now going to do a unique work in the life of Mary. The power of God, in the Person of the Holy Spirit, would overshadow her.*

9. How does it encourage you to know the presence of God overshadows a believer's life by the power of the Holy Spirit who dwells within them?

∽SELAH⧽

*Among all the godly Jewish maidens of that time in Palestine why did God select such a humble peasant young woman as Mary? Her choice by God to be the mother of the Incarnate Son is as mysterious as her conception of Him within her virgin womb. When the fullness of time had come for Jesus to be manifested He did not go to a city, but to a remote and inconsiderate town—not to a palace but a poor dwelling; not to the great and learned but to lowly partisans— for a woman to bring the Savior into a lost world. The gentle and lowly Mary of Nazareth was the Father's choice as the mother of His beloved Son, and that she herself was overwhelmed at God's condescending grace in choosing her is evident from her song of praise in which she magnified Him for regarding her lowly estate, and in exalting her.*

All the Women of the Bible

10. Why do you think God chose Mary to be the mother of Jesus?

11. Mary responds to God as His *maidservant*. A *maidservant* is a female bond-slave without any ownership rights of her own. Bond-slave is used with the highest dignity in the New Testament speaking to believers who willingly live under Christ's authority as His devoted followers. (Helps Word Studies)

    **Mary sees herself as a *maidservant* of God. What does this reveal to us about her character?**

12. What would you have to change in your attitude and actions to be a *maidservant*?

# Mary's Struggle

*Self-love is the cesspool out of which oozes every other perversion of the human heart, for ultimately everyone and everything else becomes expendable in the pursuit of its insatiable lust. Yet the thing that is most exalted in our society is the "self."*

*Dr. Dan Hayden*

### ❧SELAH❧

*Although Mary was the earthly mother of Jesus, she was also His follower and disciple. We can be sure there were many moments in her life where she would need to surrender her "rights" as a mother to bow to the authority of her Lord and Savior.*

1. Selfishness is the attitude of being concerned with one's own interests above the interests of others. Look up the following verses and identify why Mary might struggle with her own interests as Jesus' mother.

   - Mark 3:31-35

   - Luke 2:41-50

   - John 2:1-5

2. In what ways might it have been difficult for Mary to accept the truth that she had no more claim on Jesus than anyone else?

3. Submitting our desires for our loved ones to God is not always easy. Share a struggle you may have personally experienced.

4. It would have been easy for Mary's pride to get in the way of her relationship with Jesus. What do we learn about pride in the Bible?

- Proverbs 11:2

- Proverbs 14:3

- Proverbs 16:18

- Proverbs 29:23

- James 4:1

- 1 John 2:16

5. In 2 Timothy 3:1-5, we are told that in the last days, perilous times will come. What attitudes will mark the culture?

6. The phrase, *lovers of self,* is translated in the Greek, *philautos.* In contrast to the Greek word *philadelphia,* which means, *love of the brethren, philautos* means *love of oneself.*

   **Describe some ways you see the love of self playing out in the culture today.**

7. In what areas of your life do you struggle the most with selfishness?

8. **Read John 19:25-27.** There was no harder time in Mary's life than at the cross, when she would have to relinquish once and for all her own desires for God's desires. One commentator accurately depicts the moment:

*In that moment the tremendous truth must at last have dawned upon Mary, that He who hung upon the cross was not her son; that before the world was He was; that so far from being His mother, she was herself His child. On the morning of His Resurrection Jesus did not appear first to Mary His mother, but to Mary Magdalene—surely an evidence of His matchless grace.*

   **What truths would sustain Mary during this difficult time?**

9. How should those same truths help us to have victory over selfishness?

10. Gabriel declared Mary highly favored and blessed by God because of one thing: She was chosen by God to carry Christ and so are we.

   **How will you respond as one blessed and highly favored by God, chosen to carry the truth of Jesus Christ to the world around you?**

# Mary's Victory

*But to mean it when I say that I want my life to count for His glory is to drive a stake through the heart of self - a painful and determined dying to me that must be a part of every day I live.*

Louie Giglio

**Read Luke 1:39-56.**

The angel had told Mary about Elizabeth's pregnancy in Luke 1:36. So when the angel departed it is no surprise that Mary would visit her close relative who was both a strong believer and *also* expecting her first son by a miraculous birth announced by an angel.

1. How did Elizabeth encourage Mary and what was her response?

### ∙ SELAH ∙

*In Luke 1:46-55 we find a priceless treasure, **Mary's Magnificat**. This is the name given to her outpouring of song and praise to the Lord. Mary has fully surrendered her own concerns to trust and rejoice in God's plan. In her song we discover the secrets to being victorious over selfishness.*

2. Mary's song of praise is all about God's greatness. In what ways is it important that our lives be **all about Him** and **not all about us**?

3. Find a new favorite Scripture that focuses on God's greatness and write it out. Commit it to memory for the future.

4. Read Luke 1:46-47. Look up and write out the definition of the word **magnify**.

5. Share some ways you can **magnify** the Lord and take the focus off of you.

6. In Luke 1:47, Mary is rejoicing in God her Savior and the salvation that will come through Jesus Christ. Read Psalm 103:1-5 and allow praise for God to arise as you consider His benefits. Write your own song of praise thanking God for your salvation.

7. Mary refers to herself in Luke 1:48 as "lowly". She prophesies that Jesus will scatter the proud and exalt the lowly. An attitude of humility will always triumph over selfishness. What do you learn about humility from the example of Jesus in Philippians 2:1-11?

8. What important truth are we taught about humility in 1 Peter 5:5-7?

9. God's grace was there for Mary and will be there for us too when we humble ourselves. Share a time that you humbled yourself and God's grace sustained you.

10. Read Luke 1:49. What great things has the Lord done for you?

11. How can an attitude of gratitude help us to be victorious over selfishness?

*Mary's song reveals a young heart and mind thoroughly saturated with the Word of God. Her prayer resonates with Hannah's prayers (1 Samuel 1:11, 2:1-10), and includes references to the law, the psalms and the prophets.*

12. Luke 2:19 tells us that after the birth of Jesus, Mary **pondered** many things in her heart. Look up the definition of the word **pondered** and explain what it means to **ponder** the Word of God.

13. How does saturating our mind with the Word of God and pondering its deep truth help us to understand and trust in God's plan for our lives?

14. Acts 1:12-14 proves that Mary was victorious over selfishness. How are you encouraged by what you discover?

15. **What have you learned from Mary, mother of Jesus, her story, her struggle and her victory over selfishness?**

*Blessed is she who believed,*
*for there will be a fulfillment of those things*
*which were told her from the Lord.*

*Luke 1:45*

# Week 2

## *Elizabeth*

### Victorious over Discouragement

There is a well known story that describes a time the devil decided to go out of business – imagine that! But as the fable goes, the devil would offer all of his tools for sale to whoever would pay his price. On the night of the sale they were all attractively displayed: Malice, Hatred, Envy, Jealousy, Sensuality, and Deceit. A man who happened to stop by noticed another item. It was a harmless looking wedge-shaped tool and he noticed it had a lot of wear on it. The man asked the devil what it was, and he answered, **"That is Discouragement."**

"Why do you have it priced so high?"

"Because," replied the devil, "it is more useful to me than any of the others."

"I can pry open and get inside a woman's heart with discouragement, when I can not get near her with any other tool. Once inside her heart, I can use her in whatever way suits me best. Yes, the tool of discouragement is well worn because I use it with almost everyone. Very few people know it belongs to me."

Discouragement is a powerful tool used by Satan and often we do not recognize that it comes directly from His workshop. Women pay a high price when they buy into the lies of the enemy of discouragement. The word "discourage" means to "deprive of courage, hope or confidence", "to dishearten or dispirit". *When we feel discouraged, we feel like giving up.*

Are there days when you feel discouraged?

- Days when nothing you do seems to matter and you wonder why you bother
- Days when the struggles and trials of life weigh heavy upon your heart
- Days when life just seems too hard
- Days when the future appears hopeless

Like us, Elizabeth may have encountered many days of discouragement. Luke's gospel teaches us that she and her husband were well advanced in years and childless. But despite her barrenness, Scripture also tells us that Elizabeth remained righteous before God, walking in all His commandments and ordinances. The Word describes her as blameless! Out of her heartbreak, sorrow and unanswered prayer, grew a woman who brought blessing and encouragement into the lives of others.

There are hidden treasures in Elizabeth's life just waiting to be uncovered; moments that we want to examine and study closely to reap the benefits of her experience to *discover how she became victorious over discouragement.*

# Elizabeth's Story

*Elizabeth was of the daughters of Aaron and the wife of the priest, Zacharias of the division of Abijah (1 Chronicles 24:10) and mother of John the Baptist. She was related to Mary, the earthly mother of Jesus Christ (Luke 1:36). Since Mary's father was from the tribe of Judah the tie between the families must have been on Mary's mother side. We know that names in the Bible provide great insight into a person's character. So it is true with Elizabeth. According to Hitchcock's Bible Name Dictionary, Elizabeth's name means "the oath or fullness of God."*

**Read Luke 1:5-25.**

1. As a priest Zacharias would have considered Leviticus 21:7 before marrying Elizabeth. What do you learn about Elizabeth from this verse?

2. What more do you learn about her character in Luke 1:6?

3. What do we learn about being **blameless** from the following Scriptures?

   - Job 1:1

   - Psalm 18:23-25

   - Proverbs 28:10

   - Philippians 2:14-16

   - Colossians 1:21-23

   - 1 Thessalonians 5:23-24

## ❧SELAH❧

*Though Zacharias and Elizabeth were not sinless, they were blameless; nobody could charge them with any open scandalous sin; they lived honestly and inoffensively, as priests and ministers of God. In a culture in which children were considered the blessing of the Lord, and the death rate was so high that each couple had to have 5 children to keep the population number stable, being barren was considered a curse. In fact, the situation highlights the character of Zacharias, who was no doubt under pressure to divorce Elizabeth. There were people who considered it a religious duty to divorce a barren wife.*

4. Scholars believe that Elizabeth was in her sixties when she became pregnant. Her prayers for a child would have gone unanswered for many years. Why would it have been easy for Elizabeth to become discouraged?

5. Share a time when you were discouraged because God did not answer your prayers.

6. Luke 1:13 reveals through the angel's message to Zacharias, this couple's prayers had been answered. Elizabeth would bear a son whom they would call John. What beautiful promises are prophesied over their future son in Luke 1:13-17?

7. What was Zacharias' response to the angel in Luke 1:18-22 and why is he unable to speak?

8. Describe a possible connection between unbelief and discouragement.

9. Have you ever prayed to God without believing that He would really come through for you? Why or why not?

*We don't know why Elizabeth kept herself hidden for five months, but it meant that no one else knew of her pregnancy. Instead of rushing out to tell everyone she directed her thoughts to the Lord in praise. He had seen her! He had taken notice of her! He had taken away her reproach!*

10. Read Luke 1:25. **Reproach** means **disgrace** or **shame**. Jesus came to set us free from sin and death and to cleanse us from all unrighteousness. He has redeemed us completely, taking away our shame and disgrace.

    **Elizabeth would have held the truth of Psalm 34:4-5 close to her heart. Write out these verses. How do they encourage you today?**

# Elizabeth's Struggle

*We aren't told in the Bible how Elizabeth may have struggled with discouragement on days when her thoughts were drawn to what "she didn't have". But being that she was a woman just like you and me, we can be sure there were days where she would have to fight off discouragement.*

1. Describe some of the symptoms of discouragement found among the men and women in the Bible.

    • Ruth 1:20, 21 (Naomi)

    • 1 Samuel 1:7, 10 (Hannah)

    • 1 Kings 19:4 (Elijah)

    • Psalm 42:5 (David)

2. Record a time in your life that discouragement brought about similar symptoms.

3. Satan has a tool belt full of tactics. What important warning must we heed in 2 Corinthians 2:11 as it concerns the enemy's devices?

### ≈SELAH≈

In Kay Arthur's book, As Silver Refined, Kay highlights five strategies of the enemy. They are easy to identify and remember because they all begin with the letter "**D**". She rightly titles these devices used by the enemy **The Five Deadly D's**; **D**isappointment, **D**iscouragement, **D**ejection, **D**espair, and **D**emoralization.

Kay explains further:

*Together these five Deadly D's form a downward spiral of deepening defeats and disorder. They are part of a devastating plunge that's triggered when we respond wrongly to the disappointments that God in His loving sovereignty allows in our lives. Disappointment comes when our expectations aren't met. We become unhappy. When we don't conquer that disappointment in God's way, than we spin downward into discouragement, we are without courage. We want to give up. We want to quit because we're disheartened. We're ready to run rather than deal with the situation. Depression then sets in its' first degree – dejection – a lowness of spirit, a feeling of spiritual and emotional fatigue. If not reversed this dejection takes us down even further, plunging us into despair and finally into utter demoralization. At this stage of descent, hope is entirely abandoned and is replaced by apathy and numbness. Fear becomes overwhelming and paralyzing and can degenerate further into disorder and reckless action that is heedless of consequences…these are the tactics that Satan is using to defeat so many of God's children today.*

***It is important to note that when we don't conquer disappointment in our lives, we spin downward into discouragement. Discouragement causes us to focus on our problems rather than God.***

4. The Bible teaches us in Proverbs 13:12 that hope deferred makes the heart sick. Share a time that you experienced a sorrow that came from being disappointed.

5.  We often don't recognize the tool of discouragement as coming from Satan. He fuels **thoughts** that cause us to believe that our problems are bigger than God is. The prophet Jeremiah wrote the Bible's Old Testament book of Lamentations. It is a series of emotional laments over the serious spiritual and moral condition of God's people during that time. Jeremiah aka "the weeping prophet" battled with **all five of the Deadly D's** throughout his difficult ministry.

    **Describe the thoughts that weighed him down in Lamentations 3:1-20.**

6.  Jeremiah knew what **thoughts** to return to when discouragement and despair got the best of him. These truths brought him hope.

    **Describe the truths that brought Jeremiah hope in Lamentations 3:21-26.**

7.  The years of waiting for a child may have caused Elizabeth's hope for a child to fade. After all, Zacharias was unable to believe the angel when he brought the news that they could have a child. Despite a loss of hope, Elizabeth and Zacharias remained dedicated to God. Their commitment to God was not based on what He had done (or not done) but on their love for Him.

    **How can a loss of hope cause us to walk away from the Lord?**

8.  Have you walked away from the Lord in a time of hopelessness? If your answer is no, what truths about God kept you walking with Him? Use Scripture to support your answer.

9. Elizabeth and Sarah shared the same disappointment, ***but not the same response***. Elizabeth would have read and studied Sarah's life. How do you think Sarah's story influenced Elizabeth?

10. How do you sympathize with Elizabeth's struggle?

# *Elizabeth's Victory*

*Once I knew only darkness and stillness - my life was without past or future - but a little word from the fingers of another fell into my hand that clutched at emptiness, and my heart leaped to the rapture of living.*

Helen Keller

**Read Luke 1:39-45.**

1. We learn from Luke 1:41 that Elizabeth was a woman who was filled with the Holy Spirit. What does it mean to be "spirit filled"? Use Scripture to support your answer.

2. Elizabeth walked in the truth of Romans 15:13. She kept on believing in God and His Word and hope abounded in her life. How are you encouraged by the truth that hope abounds by the power of the Holy Spirit?

3. Elizabeth's life was marked by the promise she shared with Mary in Luke 1:45. Write out this promise and share how you will immediately apply it.

4. Like Elizabeth and Mary, we are victorious over discouragement when we believe that the promises of God will be fulfilled in our lives. What do we learn about the promises of God in 2 Corinthians 1:20 and 2 Peter 1:4?

23

5. Imagine Mary's state of mind upon her visit to Elizabeth. Thoughts of uncertainty and fear would capture her mind. Hearing Elizabeth's account and seeing her pregnant must have been a wonderful encouragement to Mary. Through Elizabeth, God gave Mary a personal confirmation that His word to her was indeed true! This encouragement led Mary to burst out with a song of praise. *Encouragement is the best remedy for discouragement!*

   **Look up the definition of the word "encouragement". What are some ways we can encourage ourselves and others in the Lord?**

### ☙SELAH☙

*The gift of "encouragement" or "exhortation" is found in Paul's list of gifts in Romans 12:7-8. The word translated "encourage" or "exhortation" is the Greek word "paracletos" or "paraclete" which basically means to call to one's side. "Paracletos" can have several meanings, including exhort, urge, encourage and comfort. It is interesting to note that the Holy Spirit is referred to as the "Paraclete". A person with the gift of encouragement can use this gift in both a public and private setting. It can be seen in counseling, discipleship, mentoring and preaching. The body of Christ is built up in the faith as a result of those with the ministry of encouragement.*

6. God will often use us to bring a personal confirmation of His Word to someone who needs it. When was the last time a friend encouraged you, or you encouraged a friend, with the Word of God?

7. It has been said that *"True friends lift our wings when we forget how to fly."* Ecclesiastes 4:9-12 reveal important truths that can help us to be victorious over discouragement. What do you discover?

**Read Luke 1:59-66.**

8. Despite the pressure of many to name her son after his father, Elizabeth remained obedient to the prophecy spoken over her son by the angel in Luke 1:13. This peek into her life shows us that her faith in the Word of God and her obedience to it was crucial to overcoming discouragement.

   **How does Joshua 1:7-8 support this truth?**

24

9. Mary stayed with Elizabeth and Zechariah for three months and it is very possible she was there to share in the joy of John the Baptist's birth. Elizabeth served as a great mentor to Mary. Look up the word **mentor** in a dictionary and describe some ways Elizabeth may have mentored Mary in their time together.

10. In what ways can a mentor help us to be victorious over discouragement?

11. Share a time that God used a mentor to encourage you. If you want a mentor, spend some time praying that God would bring just the right person.

12. **What have you learned from Elizabeth's story, her struggle and her victory over discouragement?**

*And coming in that instant she gave thanks to the Lord, and spoke of Him to all those who looked for redemption in Jerusalem.*

*Luke 2:38*

# Week 3

## *Anna*

### Victorious over Loneliness

*Loneliness was the first thing that God's eye named not good.*

*John Milton*

*I don't like coming home to my apartment. It's cold and dark. The first thing I do is turn on the television just to hear some human voices. I eat alone, flip channels, maybe do a little reading, and then go to bed. I've been in and out of relationships, and none of them turned out well. I see couples in the mall walking hand-in-hand, and my heart longs for someone to share my life.*

It is certainly true that women who are unmarried, divorced or widowed are more likely to encounter loneliness simply because they are more likely to be alone. However, loneliness can also occur when a marriage relationship doesn't produce the intimacy a woman expects. God has created a need in each one of us to be loved and belong and there are seasons of life that take us through lonely times, whether we are single or married. Consider the family who relocates to a new area, leaving their close friends behind. They find it difficult to develop new friendships. The student away at college, a spouse in the military, loneliness can find its way into anyone's life.

Modern technology has not helped in making it easier to develop relationships with others. Texting, e-mail and Facebook make it convenient to communicate with our friends without ever leaving our homes. On-line shopping and even church services watched from our laptops subtly work to foster an atmosphere of isolation.

Dr. Gary Collins, who is a professor of psychology and a Christian author, would agree:

*We live in a loneliness producing society. Isn't that interesting? A loneliness producing society, where rapid change and modern technology discourage intimacy and stimulate loneliness. Even in homes and churches people avoid each other, only to throw themselves blindly into open sharing with strangers.*

The enemy of our souls uses technology and a number of other tactics to isolate believers. We must be aware of his plot to keep the "lonely" alone. Anna spent most of the years of her life as a widow and her story is one that we can all relate to, no matter what season of life we find ourselves in. Her example and the fruitful and joy filled life that she embraced will definitely help us to ***discover how she became victorious over loneliness.***

# Anna's Story

*Luke writes that Anna was of a great age and that she was a widow of about eighty four years – which could mean that she lived to be at least a hundred years old, or she was an 84 year old widow. --- Either way she was of great age! Most Jewish girls married at the age of 13-14, and Anna's marriage had lasted only 7 years before her husband died, leaving her a widow in her early 20's and living as a widow for over 60 years.*

**Read Luke 2:36-38.**

1. Describe some ways Anna may have struggled with loneliness in her widowhood. Can you relate to her situation? Why or why not?

2. Look up the following verses and record God's heart for the widow.

   - Psalm 68:5

   - Psalm 146:9

   - James 1:27

## ⊰SELAH⊱

*Anna was the daughter of Phanuel, whose very name means the face of God. She was a member of the tribe of Asher, one of the ten "lost tribes" of Israel, which were scattered in the Assyrian captivity in 722 B.C. While the tribe as a whole never returned to Israel, Anna's family had made the journey back to their homeland. Church tradition would tell us that, "The women of the tribe of Asher were known for their beauty, which qualified them for royal and high-priestly marriage." Therefore the fact that she did not remarry is significant. As a young widow, the natural thing for Anna to have done would be to remarry. She must have had many such opportunities. As a member of the lost tribe of Asher, there must have been a strong incentive to marry and bear children, since this tribe may have been in danger of extinction.*

3. What may be some reasons that Anna never remarried?

4. Everything Scripture has to say about Anna is contained in just three verses. She is never mentioned anywhere else in the Bible, yet these three verses are enough to establish her as one of the most amazing women of the Bible. What other important information do you learn about Anna in these three verses?

5. Read Luke 2:25-35. What event is Anna able to witness along with Simeon, Joseph and Mary?

6. As a prophetess, Anna receives insight into things that normally remain hidden to ordinary people. She knew that the birth of the long awaited Messiah had come. Luke 2:38 tells us how she responded. What did she do?

7. Anna may well be the model for the righteous church widows that Paul describes in 1 Timothy 5:5. What do you learn about her character from this verse?

8. Based on what you have learned about Anna so far, how do you think she was able to conquer her loneliness?

# Anna's Struggle

*A. W. Tozer once said, "Most of the world's great souls have been lonely." Think of the godly people in Scripture who felt alone, and consider the reasons for their loneliness. Job felt alone in his troubles; Joseph, in his rejection from his family, Elijah, as a result of intense spiritual warfare; David, as a result of his enemy's relentless attacks and Jeremiah, because of his stand for the Lord.*

1. Who do we also discover experienced loneliness in Matthew 26:36-45? Describe His struggle.

2. David wrote psalms to God in times of his isolation and loneliness. Read Psalm 142. What does he confess to God in verse 4?

3. Share a time in your life that you felt like David.

4. Someone wisely cautioned that Satan is a pirate looking for a vessel without a fleet. How does loneliness leave us vulnerable to an attack by the enemy?

5. What are some of the things that loneliness can drive us to that we later regret?

6. When we sink into loneliness and allow it to do its redemptive work by embracing it, it can be a powerful teacher. Henri Nouwen writes in his book, The Inner Voice of Love, we may find our "loneliness not only tolerable," but even fruitful. How can we use times of loneliness in our lives as an opportunity to bear fruit?

7. We know from Luke 2:37 that Anna was a woman of prayer. How can prayer be a remedy to loneliness? Use Scripture to support your answer.

8. How do you respond to your struggle with loneliness?

9. Since the family was the center of Israelite society, those outside of its structure were alone and often needy. God desires to comfort the lonely. He wants us to turn to Him both as a Father and a Husband. How does Psalm 27:10 and Isaiah 54:5 support this important truth?

10. Describe how you can enjoy a relationship with God as your Father and Husband. Use Scripture to support your answer.

## Anna's Victory

*Jesus desires to meet you in your loneliness with a word of understanding and a heart of compassion. With Christ, you can be alone without feeling the sadness of loneliness. Right now, your aloneness is like an emotional desert, where the landscape is barren and all you feel is the heat of the sun and an awful thirst for companionship. Now, contrast this desert image with a garden image. Imagine yourself alone in a garden, listening to the soothing sounds of the birds and the relaxing rhythm of the wind in the trees. In the garden, you experience solitude—an entirely different sensation. Solitude brings refreshment, peace, and meaning.*

1. In what ways can you exchange your "desert" perspective for a "garden" perspective?

2. Anna's life was the temple and her church family. You might wonder if she lived and slept in the Temple. There were living quarters surrounding the Temple precincts, but no one was permitted to sleep within the Temple itself, nor were women allowed to stay there at night. Luke's point is simply that she was there at every available hour, attending every service, observing every sacrifice. She was faithful in worship and prayer each time the doors opened. Such was her life.

   **How can the family of God be a cure for loneliness? Use Scripture to support your answer.**

## ❧SELAH❧

*If we look at the structure of the temple as we study church history, we would discover that Anna would have been spending her time in the Women's Court. The Court of Women was also known as The Court of Prayer, not because it was only reserved for women, but because women could proceed no further. Both men and women could enter this court, talk to priests, pray, observe the proceedings, bring their sacrifices. Women had a balcony built for them to separate them from the men. Besides being the place in the temple where the women could pray the Court of Women was the one place in the temple where all Israelites could gather.*

3. Anna is called a prophetess because it was her habit to declare the truth of God's Word to others. She may have been a teacher of the Old Testament to the women – or simply had a private ministry there in the court of women offering words of counsel and encouragement from the Hebrew Scriptures. She may have spearheaded some times of intercession and prayer. The younger women would have gleaned from her wisdom. She would have celebrated with families as they presented their children to the Lord.

   **How can you be more intentional about getting involved with the women at your church to overcome loneliness?**

4. It is certainly easy as we age to lose our vigor and zest for life. The world places great emphasis on **retirement**. Many an older woman may comment "I have done my time". Is this position biblical? Explain your answer.

5. Today we might find women Anna's age playing bridge, browsing antique stores, or watching a lot of television.

   **Anna knew the truth of Psalm 84:1-2. What kept her going?**

6. Anna lived in response to Paul's encouragement in 1 Corinthians 7:34. How does Paul encourage single women to live?

### ⤋SELAH⤌

*Anna's hopes and dreams were full of the expectation of Jesus' birth. She knew the Old Testament promises and she understood that salvation from sin and the future blessing of Israel depended upon the coming of Christ. Anna's longing and hope of Christ was suddenly fulfilled as she went about her normal routine in the temple. Had she not been in the temple she would have missed out on seeing this amazing promise of God fulfilled right before her very eyes. Had she not been in the temple, she would have missed Christ.*

7. How do we miss out on Christ when we choose to isolate ourselves from the Body of Christ?

8. Anna's loneliness could have been a hindrance to her walk, yet her faith in the hope of Christ's birth kept her alive and serving Him. How should our faith in the return of Christ keep us from our struggle with loneliness?

9. Write out the words of Luke 2:38. How will you speak of Jesus to those in your sphere of influence who need redemption?

10. Imagine a conversation with Anna over a cup of tea or coffee. She is looking back on her life and sharing valuable life lessons with you. When you are finished reading this dramatic presentation, write your response to Anna.

*So Christ was offered once to bear the sins of many. To those who eagerly wait for Him He will appear a second time, apart from sin, for salvation.*

*~Hebrews 9:28~*

*I listened intently to the conversation that was taking place between the priest and these young parents. My ears were delighted to hear the words of my good friend, priest Simeon who declared, "Bless God! Mine eyes have seen thy salvation which thou hast prepared before the face of all people; a light to lighten the Gentiles, and the glory of thy people Israel." His words thrilled my heart, and he continued, "This child is set for the fall and rising again of many in Israel; and for a sign which shall be spoken against; (Yea, a sword shall pierce through thy own soul also,) that the thoughts of many hearts may be revealed."*

*This was it! Oh we had waited so many centuries and the day had come! Part of my heart was thrilled, so thrilled I could hardly contain myself. Another part of my heart broke for this young mother. Simeon's words were not all pleasant. He would fall, her heart would be pierced with pain, but God's people and the Gentiles as well would ultimately receive the blessing of salvation, just as God had promised Abraham so many centuries ago.*

*I could not wait any longer. As Simeon finished his portion of the ceremony, I burst into the room and just as one mute from birth receiving his voice for the very first time; I suddenly shouted praise to our God. I couldn't stop speaking about the wonderful gift of God's salvation. Finally, I had found my moment of prophecy, my great opportunity to bring glory to Jehovah!*

*I thought God's great fulfillment of my purpose would come in the form of a husband who died prematurely, or of the fruit of my womb, which never seemed to come to pass. But now it all made sense. God had spent all of those years shaping me for this one great assignment. After decades of walking along the stones and steps of the Temple portico, I ventured out with a new mission and passion. It was my assignment... my privilege to tell everyone that redemption was nigh!*

*I've felt the pain of loss. I've felt the struggle of waiting. I've strained to re-capture that still, small voice and I can testify at the end of that entire struggle... Jesus is so worth waiting for!*

*In my years of loneliness, He had become my best friend. In my years of hoping, He had become the true object of my hope. In my desire to matter, His glory had become my ultimate mission on earth.*

*To you who wait still upon His provision, upon His timely intervention into your pain, remember the words of another prophet... "They that wait upon the Lord shall renew their strength. They shall mount up with wings as eagles. They shall run and not be weary, they shall walk and not faint!" Teach me, Lord, to wait upon You!*

Write your response to Anna here.

11. **What have you learned from Anna's story, her struggle and her victory over loneliness?**

And He said to her,
"Daughter, your faith has made you well.
Go in peace, and be healed of your affliction."

Mark 5:34

# Week 4

## *The Woman with the Issue of Blood*

### Victorious over Suffering

We are certainly living in the last days. It is becoming more difficult to stand in faith as darkness fills the world. Sometimes the pain we experience seems like it is just too much for us to bear. We may wonder where God is when a loved one is diagnosed with cancer or when bad things happen to good people. This question and others like it can trouble the strongest believer when suffering enters her life.

God's plan for us was to live in paradise with Him forever, but because of man's sin, death and destruction came into the world. There will always be death and evil on this earth until Jesus comes back. Innocent people will continue to suffer at the hands of evildoers and sickness will take loved ones from this earth, but God's justice and purpose will always prevail. We must remember that our life on this earth is not the end and believe that God will use for good all that comes against us.

The suffering in our own lives, or in the lives of those we love, may tear at our heart, but our strength must come from the hope that God has given us. How do we live victoriously in the midst of suffering? First, we open our Bibles and look to those women who have suffered before us. ***Times may have changed, but suffering has not.***

The woman with the issue of blood suffered in many ways. Imagine a menstrual flow that would last one month or even six months. You might even be able to comprehend a year or even five years, but certainly not twelve long years. And her flow was anything but normal. All three gospel accounts reveal this woman's condition was one of continual bleeding. The Greek word used to describe her illness can be translated "hemorrhage". Also consider that she lived without the convenience of modern day toiletries and sanitation!

Her physical suffering was only a part of her problem. Being ostracized from society and living with her painful secret was the greater issue, a pain that drove her to utter despair. Our pain and suffering can easily drive us into darkness and despair. It has the potential to destroy our lives and more importantly, our relationship with God.

Because of that danger, we want to closely identify with the woman with the issue of blood; study her not from afar, but up close and personal. God has included her story in three of the Gospels and left her nameless – not because her life was not important, but so that we would understand her story represents our stories. Be vulnerable and ready to follow her into a place of health and healing. Diligently seek God through her life and ***discover how she became victorious over suffering.***

.

# Her Story

**Read Mark 5:25-34.**

To better understand this woman's story, read this dramatic paraphrase written by Ann Spangler in her book, Women of the Bible.

*The woman hovered at the edge of the crowd. Nobody watched as she melted into the throngs of bodies – just one more bee entering the hive. Her shame faded, quickly replaced by a rush of relief. No one had prevented her from joining in. No one had recoiled at her touch. She pressed closer, but a noisy swarm of men still blocked her view. She could hear Jairus, a ruler of the synagogue, raising his voice above the others, pleading with Jesus to come and heal his daughter before it was too late.*

*Suddenly the group in front of her shifted, parting like the rivers of the Jordan before the children of promise. It was all she needed. Her arm darted through the opening, fingers brushing the hem of His garment. Instantly, she felt a warmth spread through her, flushing out the pain, clearing out the decay. Her skin prickled and shivered. She felt strong and able, like a young girl coming into her own – so glad and giddy, in fact, that her feet wanted to rush her away before she created a spectacle by laughing out loud at her quiet miracle.*

*But Jesus blocked her escape and silenced the crowd with a curious question: "Who touched me?" "Who touched Him? He must be joking!" Voices murmured. "People are pushing and shoving just to get near Him!"*

*Shaking now, the woman fell at His feet. "For twelve years, I have been hemorrhaging and have spent all my money on doctors but have only grown worse. Today, I knew that if I could just touch your garment, I would be healed." But touching she knew, meant spreading her defilement – even to the rabbi.*

*Twelve years of loneliness. Twelve years in which physicians had bled all of her wealth. Her private affliction becoming a matter of public record – every cup she handled, every chair she sat on could transmit defilement to others. Even though her impurity was considered a ritual matter rather than an ethical one, it had rendered her an outcast, making it impossible for her to live with a husband, bear a child, or enjoy the intimacy of friends and family. Surely the rabbi would censure her. But instead of scolding and shaming her, Jesus praised her. "Daughter, your faith has healed you. Go in peace and be freed from your suffering."*

*His words must have been like water breaching a dam, breaking through her isolation, setting her free. He had addressed her not harshly, but tenderly, not as "woman" or "sinner" but rather as daughter. She was no longer alone, but part of His family by virtue of her faith.*

*That day countless men and women had brushed against Jesus, but only one had truly touched Him. And instead of being defiled by contact with her, His own touch had proven the more contagious, rendering her pure and whole again.*

1. According to Leviticus 15:25, how would society label the woman with the issue of blood? What additional information do you learn in Leviticus 15:27?

⊰SELAH⊱

*Most likely, this woman was unmarried, for no husband would stay with a continually unclean wife. A "flow of blood" effectively meant that a woman could not leave home, not have intercourse with her husband or any normal social contact, much less any religious activity. In effect, this woman has been excluded by her society for twelve years.*

Bonnie Thurston – Women in the New Testament

2. Share a time of suffering where you may have felt weak, incurable, destitute, untouchable, isolated, or unloved.

3. Read Mark 5:25-26 and describe this woman's search for healing.

4. **DESPERATE** is the word almost unanimously used among commentators and other Bible study resources to describe this woman with the issue of blood. The word **desperation** comes from the word **despair** which can also mean "extremely intense" or "suffering" or "driven by great need or distress". Where did her desperation eventually lead her?

5. What are some things women turn to when they are desperate?

6. What happened in Mark 5:29 when the woman with the issue of blood reached out to touch Jesus?

7. Why do you think Jesus called for this woman to identify herself?

8. How does she respond?

9. Mark 5:34 reveals the relationship between the woman with the issue of blood and Jesus. What is it?

10. What is it about this woman's story that draws you in?

# Her Struggle

1. This desperate woman suffered at the hands of the very people that should have been helping her. She had exhausted all of her resources and not only was she not better she was worse! How does Luke 8:43 support this truth?

**◈SELAH◈**
In the **Miracles of Jesus**, Leslie Flynn writes,

*"The Talmud lists at least eleven cures for this trouble, then common in Palestine. Though some astringents likely proved helpful in stanching or (holding back) the flow of blood, other remedies were such superstitious acts as carrying the ashes of an ostrich egg in a linen bag in summer and a cotton rag in winter. To get rid of this debilitating sickness, she had tried every imaginable cure but without success, she was a perpetual menstruant.*

2.  The woman with the issue of blood tried every imaginable cure. If we are being honest, you and I would admit we have often chased after a **cure**, seeking relief from our suffering. Give some examples.

3.  Why are the world's cures destined to disappoint?

4.  There is great evidence to suggest that this woman had come to the end of herself. She had come to the end of all her worldly options. She was being crushed by the weight of an illness that had plagued her for 12 long years.

    **Do you believe that God has a purpose in our suffering? Why or why not? Use Scripture to support your answer.**

∾SELAH∾

*Coming to the end of ourselves and our worldly options, along with a crushing by the weight of our suffering, represents a picture of **brokenness**. What is **brokenness**? **Brokenness** is that place where we realize that all the things we counted on to make life work, don't. **Brokenness** often happens when we've crossed over the line of what we can handle on our own, leaving us with nowhere else to turn.*

5.  Based on what you have just studied, share a time in your life when you were broken.

6. Using a dictionary look up and define **affliction**. Scripture uses this word to describe suffering. To be **afflicted** also carries the idea of **bowing down** and **being humbled**. Often we want to circumvent the process of suffering and avoid being humbled. We look for every kind of shortcut, seeking temporary relief. What does Scripture teach us about affliction?

- Psalm 119:67

- Isaiah 49:13

- Isaiah 53:4

- Jonah 2:2

7. What are some ways Satan gains the victory when we seek to "shortcut" our suffering?

8. The woman with the issue of blood desperately needed a miracle from Jesus.

- It took an act of her will to get up from the bed where she was racked with weakness and pain.
- It took an act of her will to come out into public and risk being seen among the people who had considered her "unclean".
- It took an act of her will to push her way through the crowds.
- It took an act of her will to reach out and touch the hem of His garment.
- It took an act of her will to respond to Jesus as He called her out and to make a full confession of the sin and pain in her life before a large crowd who had shunned her.

If this woman **would have given in to how she "felt" she would have missed an encounter with Jesus. How can our emotions be a detriment to our suffering?**

9. In a moment of complete and utter despair, the woman with the issue of blood reaches by faith to believe if she just touches the hem of Jesus' garment she will be healed. Describe what was meant by the hem of His garment in Deuteronomy 22:12.

10. Touching the tassels on Jesus' robe meant that she understood what they stood for – the Torah, the law given by Moses. This part of the robe was considered as most holy. Upon brushing the hem of His robe, her bleeding stopped immediately and the flow of her blood was dried up. This was a measurable, verifiable miracle. She knew that it was not the robe itself that had healed her, but the Person who wore it.

**Do you believe Jesus still performs miracles today? Why or why not?**

*Her Victory*

*To be broken is the beginning of revival. It is painful, it is humiliating, but it is the only way.*

Roy Hession

1. You and I will never meet God in revival until we first meet Him in desperation and brokenness. Like the woman with the issue of blood, your first step to victory over suffering is to admit that you can't handle life on your own. ***Don't resist being broken***.

**What does Psalm 34:18 and Isaiah 57:15 teach us about brokenness?**

◆SELAH◆
*Brokenness is a lifestyle of agreeing with God about the true condition of your heart and life, as He sees it. It is a lifestyle of unconditional, absolute surrender of your will to the will of God--a heart attitude that says, "Yes, Lord!" to whatever God allows in your life. When Jesus asked and looked around to see who had touched Him this woman responded by falling down before Jesus and telling Him the whole truth.*

2. What do you think she told Jesus? What do you need to tell Jesus?

3. If you have ever broken anything valuable, like a good piece of china or your favorite crystal, it probably ended up tossed in the trash. That's because in our minds broken things *lose* their value. But God doesn't toss aside broken things. He values them. They are priceless. He remakes them and uses them for His glory. God allows defeat, setback, adversity, or tragedy to bring us to the end of self. In the process He makes us more and more like Christ.

   **What more do you learn about this process in Jeremiah 18:3-4?**

   **Are you cooperating with the Potter? Why or why not?**

4. Jesus knew who touched Him, yet He wanted to draw this woman to Himself. Her physical healing was secondary to the relationship that He desired to have with her. He recognized her need for spiritual healing and sympathized with her plight. He knew her pain, her shame, and the condemnation she had suffered. The people surrounding her had ostracized her for twelve long years. *She came to know Jesus as her sympathetic High Priest.*

   **What do we learn from Hebrews 4:15 and 16 that can help us to be victorious in our suffering?**

5. In Mark 5:34 Jesus calls this woman **daughter** in front of the crowd. What is significant about this moment?

**⋰SELAH⋱**

It has been said that if we do not know and relate to God as Father, then we do not really understand the Gospel. Theologian J. I. Packer said in his classic book <u>Knowing God</u>:

*If you want to judge how well a person understands Christianity, find out how much he makes of the thought of being God's child, and having God as his Father. If this is not the thought that prompts and controls his worship and prayers and his whole outlook on life, it means that he does not understand Christianity very well at all.*

6.  Are you enjoying the Father/daughter relationship that is yours in Christ? Why or why not?

7.  How can this relationship help you to be victorious over suffering?

8.  The woman with the issue of blood had placed her trust in Jesus and now became His daughter, adopted into His family. She was no longer rejected but accepted in the Beloved.

    **What does Ephesians 1:3-14 tell us she received?**

9.  Receiving Christ's forgiveness would help this woman to forgive those who had hurt her. She was set free from all that kept her bound. Have you received Christ's forgiveness and are you able to forgive those who have wounded you? Explain.

10. *Have you ever wondered what happened to the woman with the issue of blood?* There is nothing more recorded about her in the Scriptures but church history tells us her name may have been Veronica. The name Veronica is Latin for Berenice, a Macedonian name, meaning "bearer of victory". You too are a "bearer of victory".

**Record a victory verse from Scripture that has helped you in a time of suffering.**

11. The woman with the issue of blood was physically healed but that is not always the case. Sometimes like Paul, we do not receive the physical healing we pray for. In 2 Corinthians 12:7-10, Paul shares with us a valuable truth that he learned in the midst of His suffering. What is it?

12. Read, meditate and comment on how God brings glory out of suffering as you read the testimony of Joni Eareckson Tada:

*Joni Eareckson Tada is a quadriplegic as the result of a diving accident in 1967. She was encouraged to seek healing by reading books and attending faith-healing services. The passage she claimed for herself was the promise Jesus gave to the invalid next to the pool of Bethseda. Jesus said to him matter of factly, "Get up! Pick up your mat and walk" (John 5:8). And the man was healed.*

*Despite her countless prayers and presence at faith-healing services, Joni was never healed. Thirty years later she visited Israel and the Pool of Bethseda. There she thanked God that He did not answer her prayers for healing. "I thanked God", she said, "because I would never have experienced His nearness as I have in this wheelchair for the past thirty years."*

*Since 1994, Joni's ministry, "Wheels for the World" has presented the Gospel by delivering wheelchairs and Bibles in developing countries. Her Wheels for the World ministry shares the love of Jesus Christ, extended through the gift of mobility, bringing hope, joy, and salvation to children and adults with disabilities around the world.*

13. **What have you learned from the woman with the issue of blood, her story, her struggle and her victory over suffering?**

*And many of the Samaritans of that city believed in Him*
*because of the word of the woman who testified,*
*"He told me all that I ever did."*

*John 5:39*

# The Samaritan Woman

## Victorious Over Idolatry

If you were to look up the word **idol** in your dictionary, it would be defined as *"an image or representation of a god used as an object of worship"*. But if we look in the Bible for a more accurate definition of an **idol**, we would discover that an idol is any desire that has grown into a consuming demand that rules our heart; it is something we think we must have to be happy, fulfilled, or secure.

In James 1:14-15, we are clearly taught that we are tempted to sin when we are drawn away and enticed by our own desires. When these desires are conceived, they give birth to sin and when sin is full-grown it brings forth death. Later, in chapter 4, James tells us these same desires are also the cause of the conflicts we encounter in our lives. All of our idolatrous desires entice us to sin in order to obtain what we think we must have in order to be happy. With that said, it is interesting to note what author Elyse Fitzpatrick points out regarding ***women*** and idolatry:

*Because women have been created with a specific call to relationship — to be their husbands' helpers (Genesis 2:18) — it is very easy for them to idolize and live for relationships with men, to look to men as the source of their identity and purpose. Many young women, in particular, are tempted to see themselves as having worth only if they are in a relationship with a man. This propensity toward idolizing men is easily seen in family life. How many conflicts have been occasioned by parents' restricting of contact between their daughter and a guy she thinks she just can't live without? Frequently, what girls wear, who they hang around with, and what forms of media they embrace are intrinsically tied to getting or keeping the attention and approval of boys. Protestations of Christian allegiance aside, popularity with certain guys is often our daughters' functional god.*

*Young women, like the rest of us, were created to worship. The siren song of the world entices them to believe that outward beauty, popularity, and the right boy will satisfy, but it never does — no matter how she pursues these gods, not even if she marries Mr. Right. Like us, she will never be satisfied with worshiping and serving the creation because there is a Creator who has already claimed His place as Husband. He not only deserves our worship, He's the only One grand enough to captivate our hearts and turn our futile idolatry, our chasing after the wind, into joyful worship. Our young women need to be dazzled by the beauty of their Redeemer King. They need to hear His story, His beauty, His love, His excellencies over and over again so that the images they are tempted to worship will pale in comparison.*

If the Samaritan woman were to join us in this study, she would shout out a **Yes** and **Amen**! She was all too familiar with idolizing men. We will see that Jesus went out of His way to meet her and expose her idols. This encounter would change her life forever. Join her at the well with Jesus and ***discover how she became victorious over idolatry.***

# The Samaritan Woman's Story

*Traveling from Jerusalem in the south to Galilee in the north, Jesus and his disciples took the quickest route, through Samaria. Tired and thirsty, Jesus sat by Jacob's Well, while his disciples went to the village of Sychar, about a half mile away, to buy food. It was about noon, the hottest part of the day.*

**Read John 4:1-42.**

1. In biblical times, women usually came to draw water either in the early morning or in the cool of the evening, to avoid the heat. They came together, perhaps as many as 20 or 30 at a time, carrying water jars on their heads. It would have been an opportunity to talk and enjoy fellowship. What might be some of the reasons the Samaritan woman came alone at the hottest part of the day to draw water? (Hint: John 4:18)

2. Do you think divorced women in the church face the same stigma today? Why or why not?

3. Read John 4:9. What did the Samaritan woman discover about Jesus?

4. In His encounter with the woman at the well, Jesus broke three Jewish customs:

   - *He spoke to a woman (Rabbis did not even speak to their own wives or daughters in public.)*
   - *He spoke to a Samaritan (a group the Jews traditionally despised)*
   - *He drank from the cup of water she provided which would make Him ceremonially unclean.*

   **What do you value about Jesus' heart toward the Samaritan woman?**

5. Jesus is talking about **water** that the Samaritan woman knew nothing about. What does John 7:37-38 teach us about **living water**?

6. 1 Corinthians 2:14 explains why the Samaritan woman could not understand what Jesus meant by **living water**. What do you discover?

## ❧SELAH❧

*Water for drinking is one of the symbols of the Holy Spirit in the Bible. (Water for washing is a symbol of the Word of God; see John 15:3 and Ephesians 5:26.) Just as water satisfies thirst and produces fruitfulness, so the Spirit of God satisfies the inner person and enables us to bear fruit. Jesus offered the Samaritan woman living water and eternal satisfaction!*

*Bible Exposition Commentary*

7. The Samaritan woman was thirsty and brought her empty jar to the well to be filled with water. Little did she know that her own emptiness would be filled with living water!

   **What emptiness do you need to bring to Jesus today so that He can fill you with the Holy Spirit?**

8. Describe the Samaritan woman's idol.

9. Whether we are single, divorced, widowed or married, the tendency to make men an idol is equally present. Do you agree? State your case.

10. Jesus confronts the Samaritan woman with her sin and she abruptly changes the subject. How do you respond when the Holy Spirit reveals the idols in your life?

# The Samaritan Woman's Struggle

*Idolatry is the practice of seeking the source and provision of what we need either physically or emotionally in someone or something other than the one true God. It is the tragically pathetic attempt to squeeze life out of lifeless forms that cannot help us meet our real needs.*

Scott J. Hafemann

1. What are some of the idols promoted in the culture today?

2. How does the enemy use these idols to set people on a path of destruction?

3. Read Isaiah 44:9-20 and record everything Isaiah teaches us about idols.

4. How do we see these truths playing out in the life of the Samaritan woman?

**∾SELAH∾**

*Just as a fisherman looking for fish knows to go where the water is roiling, look for your idols at the bottom of painful emotions, especially those that never seem to lift and that drive you to do things you know are wrong. If you are angry, ask, "Is there something here too important to me, something I am telling myself I have to have at all costs?" Do the same thing about strong fear or despair and guilt. Ask yourself "Am I so scared, because something is being threatened, which I think is a necessity when it is not? Am I so down on myself because I have lost or failed at something which I think is a necessity when it is not?" If you are over-working, driving yourself into the ground with frantic activity, ask yourself, "Do I feel that I must have this thing to be fulfilled and significant?" When you ask questions like that, when you "pull your emotions up by the roots," as it were, sometimes you will find your idols clinging to them.*

*Timothy Keller*

5.  Take a moment to ponder the above commentary and respond with an examination of your own life.

    - *Is there something you are telling yourself you have to have at all costs?*
    - *Is there something you feel you must have in order to be fulfilled and significant?*
    - *What idols might you be clinging to?*

6.  1 John 5:21 teaches us to keep ourselves from idols. What are some practical ways we can protect ourselves from idols? Use Scripture to support your answer.

7.  What is the danger of placing expectations on people that only God can fulfill?

8.  Share a time that you placed a high expectation on a person or relationship and they failed you. What did you learn from that experience

9. Write a paragraph about what it means to walk in the truth of Mark 12:30.

10. Aren't you glad to know that Jesus loved the Samaritan woman before she loved Him? He scheduled a divine appointment to personally reveal Himself to her. When did Jesus first reveal Himself to you? Were you surprised to find out that He knew everything about you? Why or why not?

# The Samaritan Woman's Victory

*Other gods call us to bow down and worship them, to treasure them before God. How can we overcome this idolatry? The obvious antidote to idolatry is to become a worshipper of the true and living God.*

1. Read Acts 14:8-18. Lystra was full of idolatry. God uses Paul to heal a man who has been crippled since birth. The people of Lystra begin to worship Paul and Barnabas thinking that the power that healed this man somehow came from them. When Paul and Barnabas heard of what was going on they were justifiably horrified. God forbid that anything they did could be misconstrued in such a manner as to lead their hearers into even more idolatry.

**What wisdom does Paul give the people regarding idols in Acts 14:15-17?**

2. What do you learn about the Thessalonian believers in 1 Thessalonians 1:8-10?

3. What **useless** things do you need to turn from in order to turn to the living God?

4. Paul describes the attributes of God that make Him and Him alone, a fitting object of worship. He declares that God is the Creator of all things and all things are dependent upon Him for their existence. Explain how Romans 1:20 validates this truth.

5. What important truth does Jesus share with the Samaritan woman in John 4:14?

6. The Samaritan woman was thirsty but drinking from the wrong well. Jeremiah 2:13 helps us to better understand this principle. Explain.

7. Contrast the broken cisterns in Jeremiah to what you discover about God in Psalm 36:7.

8. Jesus diagnosed the great problem with the Samaritan's worship: They worshipped a God they did not know (John 4:22), therefore it was in ignorance and idolatrous. It is possible that like the Samaritan woman our perception of God is not the one true God at all.

   **What does the Lord say about Himself in Isaiah 43:10-13?**

9. In what practical ways can we come to know, believe and understand God?

.

*Jesus adds in John 4:23-24 that the time is coming when the true worshippers will worship God "in spirit and in truth", in other words, they will worship God from the heart and with true knowledge. True worship must be "in spirit," that is, engaging the whole heart. Unless there's a real passion for God, there is no worship in spirit. At the same time, worship must be "in truth," that is, properly informed. Unless we have knowledge of the God we worship, there is no worship in truth. Both are necessary for satisfying and God-honoring worship. Spirit without truth leads to a shallow, overly-emotional experience that could be compared to a high. As soon as the emotion is over, when the fervor cools, so does the worship. Truth without spirit can result in a dry, passionless encounter that can easily lead to a form of joyless legalism. The best combination of both aspects of worship results in a joyous appreciation of God informed by Scripture. The more we know about God, the more we appreciate Him. The more we appreciate, the deeper our worship. The deeper our worship, the more God is glorified.*

10. Where might you be lacking as you seek to worship God in spirit and in truth?

11. The Samaritan woman discovered the true and living God as Jesus revealed Himself to her at the well. Isaiah 12:2-6 beautifully portrays her response to Jesus. Compare these verses with John 4:28-29, 39.

12. When we are filled with living water that flows continually, our desire will be to tell everyone we know about Jesus. Are you sharing Jesus with everyone you know? Why or why not?

13. **What have you learned from the Samaritan woman's story, her struggle and her victory over idolatry?**

And Jesus said to her,
"Neither do I condemn you; go and sin no more."


John 8:11

# The Woman Caught in Adultery

## Victorious over Sexual Sin

Paul's admonition in 1 Corinthians 6:18, **to flee sexual immorality,** is needed just as much today as it was then when he addressed sexual sin in the church of Corinth.

Sexual immorality is rampant in today's culture; a culture that is filled with temptations everywhere that stir lust. As women who desire to follow Christ, it is critical that we have a clear understanding of sexual sin and its dangers. Morality today is being loosely defined and redefined, even in the church, encouraging many to engage in sinful behavior. Many believers have fallen because they underestimated the power of sexual temptation.

Gordon MacDonald, a wonderful pastor and at one time president of Inter Varsity Christian Fellowship, shares in his book Rebuilding Your Broken World about a time when he was asked about how Satan might get him. He answered:

*All sorts of ways, I suppose; but I know there's one way he wouldn't get me. "What's that?" He'd never get me in the area of my personal relationships. That's one place where I have no doubt that I'm as strong as you can get. A few years after that conversation my world broke wide open. A chain of seemingly innocent choices became destructive, and it was my fault; choice, by choice, by choice - each easier to make - each becoming gradually darker. And then my world broke -- in the very area I had predicted I was safe -- and my world had to be rebuilt.*

He goes on to quote from My Utmost for His Highest:

### *"An unguarded strength is actually a double weakness."*

Here is a godly man with a good marriage who had written books on family life and yet fell into adultery. Why? Because he thought it couldn't happen to him and left this part of his life unguarded.

It has been said that the power of sexual sin **destroys** the body, **demolishes** the home and **devastates** the soul. The woman caught in adultery would certainly agree. If it weren't for Jesus, death would have been the consequence for her sin.

Sexual sin is not to be treated lightly. Though forgiveness is possible, often the consequences of sexual immorality live on. It is of the utmost importance that we pay close attention and understand Jesus' final words to the woman caught in adultery. "**Neither do I condemn you**", words that offer healing and hope for the woman who has committed sexual sin and "**Go and sin no more**" a strong exhortation to not sin in this area again. As stones begin to be thrown, we will join this woman and *discover how we can be victorious over sexual sin.*

# Her Story

*In the presence of her accusers, she burned with shame. Against her protests, she found herself being dragged into the temple area, her face flushed with embarrassment. Caught in the very act of adultery, her secret sin was exposed for all to see.*

**Read John 7:53:8-11.**

1. Look up the word **adultery** in a dictionary and write out the definition.



2. What do the following verses from the Bible teach us about adultery?

   • Exodus 20:14

   • Mark 10:12

   • Galatians 5:19



3. What are some of the painful consequences caused by the sin of adultery?



4. Read and write out Proverbs 6:32. In what ways is the sin of adultery destructive to a woman's soul?

**◈SELAH◈**

*Adultery cuts into the fragile and vulnerable places of the heart causing indescribable pain and trauma. It annihilates trust, destroys self esteem and severs the bonds of love with the cold steel blade of betrayal. It is only a loved one, who was trusted with the deepest joys, fears, hopes and dreams that can hurt another so deeply.*

5.  Possibly feeling lonely and unloved, this woman's heart betrayed her into thinking that she could find love and safety in another man's arms. What other lies does the enemy use to tempt women to stray outside of their marriage and singleness?

6.  The men accusing the woman caught in adultery had an ulterior motive. They were bent on using her to entrap Jesus so they could accuse Him of sin. Jesus was put in a position to either disrespect the Law of Moses which would be the case if He were to say "don't stone her" or He had to disregard the Roman law, which mandated that the Jews did not have the authority to put someone to death. These men were willing to exploit this women's disgrace for their own evil purposes. They hated Jesus and hoped to bring Him to ruin.

    **Look up the word "exploited" in a dictionary. How are women in the culture today being exploited in the area of sexual sin?**

7.  What do you think Jesus wrote on the ground with His finger in John 8:6?

8.  John 8:9 reveals this woman's accusers were being convicted by their conscience. The idea that the law should be combined with an attitude of restoration and compassion never entered their minds. They wanted to make sure that every lawbreaker paid every last cent of their transgression. They were planning to murder Jesus, and were guilty of something far worse than the charge of adultery.

    **The worst sinners are often the greatest accusers. What should our attitude be towards a sister who has fallen into sin? Use Scripture to support your answer.**

9. Jesus and the woman caught in adultery are left alone to deal with her sin. Jesus does not condone what she had done, or dismiss her sin as unimportant, or understandable. He knows, and she does too, that what she has done is wrong. He condemns the sin and commands her not to sin again.

   **What do you think might have been this woman's response to her encounter with Jesus?**

10. Does your life share anything in common with the woman of adultery? Why or why not?

# Her Struggle

*The pleasures of sin deceive us like the bait hides the hook. We must call it what God calls it - sin. We want to say, "affair" but God says "adultery." We want to say, "love" but God says "lust." We want to say "sexy" but God says "sin." We want to say, "romantic" but God says "ruin." We want to say, "destiny" but God says "destruction."*

*David Guzik*

1. Read Jude 7 and compare Sodom and Gomorrah to the culture we live in today.

2. The Complete Word Study Dictionary defines the Greek word **porneia** as sexual immorality, and fornication. It is used generally to refer to any sexual sin. List the sexual sins that are mentioned in 1 Corinthians 6:9.

~s&SELAH&~

*Sexually immoral behavior is serious because of the condition of the heart and the life that is revealed by the act. A life driven to sexual sin reflects thinking that has long been infected by sensual images and self-pleasure. These thoughts may have become so common that a person is hardly aware of them. What one may know or think they know theologically and biblically is less important than the imaginations of her heart that eventually cause her to act out what she thinks.*

3. Deception attacks God-centered living through self-centered thinking and comes from within one's own heart and mind. Every sexual sin is deceitful and affects the mind so the temptation is often not recognized for what it truly is until after the sin is committed.

   **What does Scripture teach us about the dangers of self-centered thinking?**

   - Genesis 6:5

   - Psalm 10:4

   - Proverbs 12:5

   - Isaiah 59:7

   - Romans 1:21

4. Deception may come from outside sources. But regardless of the source, deception affects the mind and influences what people think about God and themselves. Satan easily leads them astray. To understand how we are deceived is one thing, but to guard against it is another.

   **What are some ways we can guard against being deceived? Use Scripture to support your answer.**

5. What do you learn about adultery in Matthew 5:27-30?

**Jesus is serious about the remedy for sexual sin in these verses. What does He tell us to do and how should that work practically in our lives?**

6. Sexual sin begins in the heart and thought life. We see this truth played out in statistics, which show that more women today are having affairs because of the Internet, specifically with the temptations of online technology.

   **How is the enemy winning with online temptation?**

7. Is there an ongoing temptation that you need to immediately cut off in your life?

## ⋖SELAH⋗

*If David had considered the cost of his sexual sin with Bathsheba, he would have seen that it was much greater than he could have ever imagined. His illicit pursuit of pleasure directly and indirectly resulted in:*

- An unwanted pregnancy
- The murder of a trusted friend
- A dead baby
- His daughter raped by his son
- One son murdered by another son
- A civil war led by one of his sons
- A son who imitates David's lack of self-control leading him and much of Israel away from God

*The same kind of ruin comes of adultery today. We think about all the children who went to bed without daddy at home because of the terrible attack on our country on September 11, 2001. But far more children go to bed every night without daddy in the house because of adultery.*

David Guzik

8.  It has been said that the power of sexual sin **destroys** the body, **demolishes** the home and **devastates** the soul. Give some examples.

    - Destroys the body


    - Demolishes the home


    - Devastates the soul


9.  The man who slept with the woman caught in adultery was very likely among her accusers. How does sexual sin cause a woman shame, embarrassment and humiliation?




10. Sexual sin is a serious matter. What does Scripture teach about the person who refuses to repent and turn from sexual sin?

    - 1 Corinthians 5:9-13


    - Ephesians 5:11


    - 2 Thessalonians 3:6


    - 1 Timothy 5:20

11. It was John Piper who said, *"The hiddenness of sexual sin does not absolve us of corporate accountability for the sexual sin in our churches"*. We can not turn a blind eye when we know a sister is living in sexual sin.

   **How does James 4:17 support this truth?**

*Neither do I condemn you; go and sin no more. - Jesus*

### ❧SELAH☙

***Neither do I condemn you*** - *These words spoken by Jesus would set the woman caught in adultery free. Though her situation was both embarrassing and humiliating, this woman's secret sin was now exposed; out in the open where she and Jesus could deal with it. She would no longer suffer with guilt and shame. If we have allowed lust and sexual sin to control our lives, we too must bring it out in the open and yield to the conviction of the Holy Spirit and repent. The stones of shame, guilt and death will be removed as we seek God's forgiveness and allow Him to cleanse us physically, emotionally and spiritually.*

1. What is the promise of Scripture for those who repent of their sins?

   • Psalm 103:12

   • Romans 6:21-23

   • Hebrews 10:22

   • 1 John 1:8-9

2.  Psalm 51 is a beautiful prayer of repentance. This psalm was written by David after Nathan the prophet confronted him with the truth of his sexual sin and the murder of Bathsheba's husband. It could be that God is using this study to confront you in the same way. Take time to confess your sexual sin before God and pray through this Psalm. Share some of the verses that minister to your heart.

### ✺SELAH✺

*You can not take back sexually what has been given any more than you can take back that which has been spoken. However, that which has been lost, your purity, can be reclaimed. As you open your heart to the Lord and as you desire His best for your life, like the woman caught in adultery, you can come to know Him as Redeemer and Restorer.*

3.  Write out the beautiful truths of healing and restoration listed below. What do these promises in Scripture reveal about the character of God?

    *   Isaiah 44:22

    *   Hosea 6:1

    *   Joel 2:12-13, 25-27

***Go and sin no more*** *– These words spoken by Jesus would challenge the woman caught in adultery to leave her sin behind and live in the new life that Christ offered her. He had saved her from death and desired that she would now live for Him. We do not know what happened to the woman caught in adultery but we can be sure that in her gratitude for what she had been spared from, she did not abuse the grace of God. We must take these final words of Jesus to heart –* ***let us go and sin no more.***

4.  What precautions can a woman take in her thought life to keep her from sexual sin? Use Scripture to support your answer.

5. The woman caught in adultery could have determined ahead of time how she would respond to sexual temptation. We read in Job 31:1 that Job had a plan in place to protect his sexual purity. What was it?

6. In what practical ways can we *make a covenant with our eyes*?

7. What important truths in 1 Corinthians 6:18-20 must we keep before us at all times as we seek to be victorious over sexual sin?

8. While Samson relied on God for physical strength, he never saw his need for strength of character. *Samson's character cost him not only his liberty, but also his life*. Unlike the carnal life of Samson, Joseph's life of integrity and self-control prove that we can have pure lives. Look up and record the biblical truths that girded Joseph's life.

   • Job 27:5

   • Psalm 66:18-19

   • Proverbs 11:6

   • Romans 12:1

   • 2 Peter 1:3

9. The Bible is full of practical steps that will help you to walk in victory over sexual sin and live a life of sexual integrity. As you carefully study each step, write out the corresponding Bible verse.

- Wear, as a reminder of your purity, a ring, necklace or bracelet. (Psalm 61:8)

- Trust God to meet your need for love. (Psalm 143:8)

- Develop a proactive strategy for countering sexual triggers. (Proverbs 4:14)

- Pray for the right accountability partner. (Proverbs 27:6)

- Write out your vow to be sexually pure from this day on. (Ecclesiastes 5:4)

- Yield to Christ, who lives in you, trusting Him to produce in you a life of purity. (John 15:3-5)

- Never put yourself in a tempting situation. (1 Corinthians 10:13)

- Transform your mind through the written word of God. (Romans 12:2)

- Find friends who hold the same commitment. (Philippians 2:2)

10. **What have you learned from the woman caught in adultery, her story, her struggle and her victory over sexual sin?**

Then Mary took a pound of very costly oil of spikenard, anointed the feet of Jesus, and wiped His feet with her hair. And the house was filled with the fragrance of the oil.

John 12:3

# Week 7

## Mary at Bethany

### Victorious over the World

*Has this world been so kind to you that you should leave with regret? There are better things ahead than any we could leave behind.*

C.S. Lewis

Every day we face constant temptation to love the world. In the Bible, the term **world** most often refers to the humanistic system that is at odds with God. When we are told not to love the world, the Bible is referring to the world's corrupt value system. Satan is the god of this world, and he has his own value system which is completely contrary to God's. Loving the world means being devoted to its treasures, philosophies, and priorities.

Max Lucado draws us a vivid picture of worldliness:

*Not long ago I boarded a plane. I walked down the aisle, found my seat, and sat down next to a strange sight. The man seated next to me was in a robe and slippers. He was dressed for the living room, not for a journey. His seat was odd, too. Whereas my seat was the cloth type you normally see, his was fine leather. "Imported," he said, when he noticed I was looking. "Bought it in Argentina and put it on myself." Before I could speak he pointed to some inlaid stones in the armrest. "The rubies I purchased in Africa. They cost me a fortune."*

*That was only the beginning. His fold-down table was of mahogany. There was a portable TV installed next to the window. A tiny ceiling fan and globed light hung above us. I had never seen anything like it. My question was the obvious one, "Why did you spend so much time and expense on an airline seat?" "I live here," he explained. "I make my home on the plane." "You never get off?"*

*"Never! How could I deboard and leave such comfort?" Incredible. The man made a home out of a mode of transportation. He made a residence out of a journey. Hard to believe? You think I'm stretching the truth? Well, maybe I haven't seen such foolishness in a plane, but I have in life. And so have you. You've seen people treat this world like it was a permanent home. It's not. You've seen people pour time and energy into life like it will last forever. It won't. You've seen people so proud of what they have done, that they hope they will never have to leave—they will. We all will. We are in transit. Someday the plane will stop and the deboarding will begin. Wise are those who are ready when the pilot says to get off. I don't know much, but I do know how to travel. Carry little. Eat light. Take a nap. And get off when you reach the city.*

It is easy to become captivated by the world. The challenge for us is to *live in the world* while **preventing the world to live in us**. This week we will meet Mary of Bethany. Her life holds the answers we desperately seek to resist the temptation to live for this world. May we be diligent in our pursuit to **discover how we can be victorious over the world.**

69

# Mary's Story

*Oh, that I could forever sit, like Mary, at the Master's feet: Be this my happy choice: my only care, delight and bliss, My joy, my Heaven on earth be this, to hear the Bridegroom's voice.*

*Charles Wesley*

**Read John 12:1-8.**

1.  What important fact do we learn about Mary's life from the following verses?

    *   Luke 10:39

    *   John 11:32

    *   John 12:3

### ❧SELAH❧

*More than anything else Mary loved to sit quietly and peacefully at Christ's sacred feet, and become lost in His unfolding of the truth. Mary, more than any other individual in the New Testament, was associated with His feet, betokening her humility, reverence and hunger for spiritual knowledge. She sat at His feet as a disciple, eager to learn of His will and word; fell at His feet in worship and grief; anointed His feet with precious ointment and wiped His feet with her lovely long hair—all of which is in keeping with her spiritual character.*

*All the Women of the Bible - Zondervan*

2.  Do you love to sit quietly and peacefully in the presence of Christ and become lost in His unfolding of the truth? Why or why not?

3.  The word **devoted** is often used to describe Mary of Bethany. Look up the word **devoted** in a dictionary and write out the definition.

4.  **Read Mary's account in Mark 14:3-9**. The disciples lacked spiritual sensitivity to what was going on yet Mary had a deeper understanding. Though she may have not perceived the full significance of what Jesus would soon face in His death, she allowed the impulses of her heart to have full expression; her devotion filled the room with a beautiful fragrance that symbolically anticipated the fragrance of Christ's death, a death that would bring salvation to the whole world.

    **How can you gain a better understanding of the deeper things of God?  Use Scripture to support your answer.**

5.  What do you learn about Mary's hair in John 12:3?

### &SELAH&

*Mary's unkempt hair would follow the custom of the Jews in times of grief and mourning. She knew that she was anointing her great Teacher for burial, that her lavish gift would cling to Him on the cross and in the tomb. Her disheveled hair was in keeping with her mourning spirit.*

6.  What is the lavish gift that you will offer Christ as a response to what He accomplished for you on the cross?

7.  List some synonyms for the word **extravagant**.

8.  Do you believe that anything done for Christ is never wasted? Why or why not?

9.  Share a time when your love for Jesus caused you to act extravagantly.

10. Mary's devotion to Jesus cost her something that she valued, but in return, she blessed generations she would never meet. How are you blessed today by Mary's devotion? What practical steps can you take to respond to her example?

# Mary's Struggle

*It has been suggested that Mary's alabaster jar filled with perfume could have been her dowry. In biblical times, a dowry might consist of money, jewelry or other valuable effects.*

1. Mary could have saved her dowry for her earthly bridegroom, but instead she chose to use it for Jesus. 2 Corinthians 4:18 suggests a reason that we place **temporal** things in front of things that have **eternal** value, what is it?

2. Write out John 12:23-26 in your own words.

3. Are you loving your life or losing it? Explain.

4. What do we learn about the dangers of loving the world in the following Scriptures?

   • Mark 4:19

   • Luke 9:25

   • James 4:4

- 1 John 2:15

5. Solomon lacked not one thing when it came to the best the world had to offer. When he came to the end of his life, he learned a sobering reality which he records for us in Ecclesiastes 2:11. Write out his conclusion in your own words.

6. The Hebrew word **hebel** translated **vanity** in Ecclesiastes 2:11 carries the idea of **emptiness.** How do the things of this world leave us empty?

7. What have you chased after in this world that left you empty?

8. What do we learn from Lot's wife in Genesis 19:26? Are there any traces of the world you are unwilling to leave behind? Explain your answer.

## ❧SELAH❧

*While the odor of the spikenard was sweet to many, it smelled of waste to others. Judas with his calculating mind quickly figured up the cost of it and called it wasted on Jesus. Today the world may consider a life wholly consecrated to Jesus as a waste. Being a single woman, the culture would have pressed Mary of Bethany to marry, but instead she committed her life to following whole-heartedly after Christ.*

9.  We see from Mary's devotion, that marriage and children are not everything. If you are a single woman, do you feel pressure from the world to get married? Why or why not?

10. No respectable woman in the culture of that time would have appeared in public with her hair unbound. But here among friends and in the presence of Jesus, Mary's love became vulnerable. Jesus' feet needed to be wiped and Mary threw caution to the wind, not worrying about what people would think about her.

    **Would you say that you are a woman who "blends" in with the culture or are you are woman who "stands out" in the culture? Explain your answer.**

11. It would have been easier for Mary to simply tell Jesus how much she loved Him, but she wanted to demonstrate it.

    **How did David describe his love for God in 1 Chronicles 21:24?**

12. Often we give the world the best of our time, energy and resources. Jesus ends up with our leftovers. What are some ways we can be intentional in giving all that we are and all that we have to Christ?

13. How will you extravagantly demonstrate your love for Christ in this season of your life?

# Mary's Victory

*If human love does not carry a man beyond himself, it is not love. If love is always discreet, always wise, always sensible and calculating, never carried beyond itself, it is not love at all. It may be affection, it may be warmth of feeling, but it has not the true nature of love in it. Have I ever been carried away to do something for God not because it was my duty, nor because it was useful, nor because there was anything in it at all beyond the fact that I love Him?*

*Have I ever realized that I can bring to God things which are of value to Him, or am I mooning round the magnitude of His Redemption whilst there are any number of things I might be doing? Not Divine, colossal things which could be recorded as marvelous, but ordinary, simple human things which will give evidence to God that I am abandoned to Him? Have I ever produced in the heart of the Lord Jesus what Mary of Bethany produced?*

*There are times when it seems as if God watches to see if we will give Him the abandoned tokens of how genuinely we do love Him. Abandon to God is of more value than personal holiness. Personal holiness focuses the eye on our own whiteness; we are greatly concerned about the way we walk and talk and look, fearful lest we offend Him. Perfect love casts out all that when once we are abandoned to God. We have to get rid of this notion - "Am I of any use?" and make up our minds that we are not, and we may be near the truth.*

*It is never a question of being of use, but of being of value to God Himself. When we are abandoned to God, He works through us all the time.*

*Oswald Chambers*

1. Based on what you have just read, have you ever been carried away?

1. It is priceless to have the very words of Jesus spoken about Mary. His words reveal not only what He loved about Mary, but they provide us with the answers we need to be victorious over the world.

    - Matthew 26:10-13

    - Mark 14:8

    - Luke 10:42

2.  The church of Ephesus was one of the great revival centers in the early church. Yet, they did not sustain freshness in their love for Jesus. What do you discover in Revelation 2:1-5 is the reason for their loss?

3.  Have you held being a worker of God above being a lover of God? Why will lovers of God always "outwork" the workers of God?

4.  Where do you need to be more like Mary in your life?

5.  We see Mary in John 11:32 weeping at the feet of Jesus, grieving the death of her brother, Lazarus. What is Jesus' response to Mary's pain in John 11:33-36?

◈SELAH◈

*Seeing Jesus at the tomb of Lazarus we get a glimpse of the deep compassion that Jesus felt for those who were suffering. Mary and Martha were broken-hearted that their brother had died. Jesus could feel the pain that Mary and Martha felt at that moment and He shed real tears for them. All the people watching could see the great love that Jesus felt for this family.*

6.  Jesus wants us to draw close to Him in our time of need. Mary didn't turn to the remedies of the world in her time of trial, but drew her strength from the depth and intimacy of her relationship with Jesus. She lived out the truths of Psalm 63:1-8.

    **What do you learn about being victorious over the world in these verses?**

7.  2 Corinthians 2:14-15 challenges us to a life like Mary's, a life with eternal impact. In what ways can we diffuse the fragrance of Christ in our spheres of influence?

8. Ephesians 5:2 commands us to walk in love as Christ loved us. He pours His love into our hearts and we pour it out to a world that desperately needs it. How does Romans 5:5 illustrate this beautiful truth?

9. Read Romans 12:1in the NASB version below.
   *Therefore I urge you, brethren, by the mercies of God, to present your bodies a living and holy sacrifice, acceptable to God, which is your spiritual service of worship.*

   **Based on Mary's example, describe in your own words what it means to be a living sacrifice.**

10. **What have you learned from Mary of Bethany, her story, her struggle and her victory over the world?**

Now when He rose early on the first day of the week,
He appeared first to Mary Magdalene,
out of whom He had cast seven demons.

Mark 16:9

# Week 8

## Mary Magdalene

### Victorious over the Darkness

According to Scripture, demon possession is a harsh reality. As our world grows darker every day, we recognize that demon possession and control did not end with the New Testament. The symptoms of demon possession today are the same as we read about in the Bible. Unusual physical strength, cutting, split personality, hearing voices, fortune telling, participation in the occult and fits of rage mark many in the culture today.

As we come to Mary Magdalene's story with a heart to be victorious over the darkness, it is important that we deeply ponder the depth of darkness from which she was delivered. Spurgeon describes her vividly:

*Mary Magdalene represents those who have come under the tormenting and distracting power of Satan, and whose lamp of joy is quenched in tenfold night. They are imprisoned not so much in the dens of sin as in the dungeons of sorrow, not so criminal as they are wretched, nor so depraved as they are desolate. We do not with any certainty understand the precise nature of being possessed with the devil. Holy Scripture has not been pleased to acquaint us with the philosophy of possessions, but we know what the outward symptoms were. Persons possessed with devils were unhappy; they found the gloom of the sepulcher to be their most congenial resort. They were unsocial and solitary. If they were permitted, they broke away from all those dear associations of the family circle which give half the charms to life: they delighted to wander in dry places, seeking rest and finding none: they were pictures of misery, images of woe. Such was the seven times unhappy Magdalene, for into her there had entered a complete band of devils. She was overwhelmed with seven seas of agony, loaded with seven manacles of despair, encircled with seven walls of fire. Neither day nor night afforded her rest, her brain was on fire, and her soul foamed like a boiling caldron. Miserable soul! No dove of hope brought the olive branch of peace to her forlorn spirit, she sat in the darkness and saw no light, her dwelling was in the valley of the shadow of death. Among all the women of Magdala there was none more wretched than she, the unhappy victim of restless and malicious demons.*

As we go about our daily lives, it is easy to forget that we are in the midst of an eternal battle, an invisible war. The same demonic spirits that Jesus confronted we encounter. In a world that no longer accepts God or a biblical worldview, the escalation of evil is easily seen in the headlines and on the news. Though Christians cannot be possessed by a demon, they can certainly be oppressed, harassed, and rendered ineffective for the Kingdom. We are targets for the enemy's destruction and we cannot afford to be dabbling in the darkness. We must fight back the darkness of depression, oppression, and sorrow and allow the light of Christ to flood our lives.

Mary Magdalene was healed from seven demons and never looked back. If she were here today, she would want to share her powerful testimony with us and pass on all that Jesus taught her. The story of her life and her journey with Christ will reveal and teach us the deep truths that will help us to ***discover how to be victorious over the darkness.***

# Mary Magdalene's Story

*Mary Magdalene's distinguishing characteristic is that she underwent an exorcism at the command of Jesus.*

1. Read Mark 5:1-5 and describe some of the symptoms of demonic possession.

2. What important information do you learn about Mary Magdalene in Mark 16:9?

3. How does this truth encourage you and testify to the power of Christ and His deliverance? Use Scripture to support your answer.

4. Put together a profile of Mary Magdalene from the following verses:

   • Matthew 27:54-61

   • Matthew 28:1

   • Mark 15:40, 47

   • Mark 16:1, 9-11

   • Luke 8:1-3

   • John 19:25

**5.** What conclusions do you draw from Mary Magdalene's profile?

**Read John 20:1-18.**

6. Describe Mary's experience at the tomb in John 20:11-18.

7. Through her tears, Mary stoops to look inside of the place where her Savior had been laid just a few days before. Two angels tell her that Jesus is not there. When she turns around to leave, she runs right into Jesus. Perhaps because she was in such deep anguish, Mary did not recognize Him. In fact, she thought He was the gardener.

   **Share a time that you may have not recognized Jesus in the midst of your pain.**

8. Mary called Jesus **Rabboni** which means **Teacher** or **Master**. What insight does this provide us about her relationship with Jesus?

9. Can you call Jesus your **Rabboni**? Is He your **Teacher** and **Master**? Why or why not?

10. While it is true that most rabbis in that culture did not normally allow women to be their disciples, Christ allowed women to be in His close circle of disciples. How does Galatians 3:28 reflect Christ's heart?

11. Mark 16:9 reveals a surprising truth. When Jesus rose from the grave He appeared **<u>first</u>** to Mary! Why do you think Jesus appeared first to Mary? Share your thoughts.

# Mary Magdalene's Struggle

*Mary Magdalene did have a dark past. Nothing indicates that her conduct was ever lewd or sordid in any way that would justify the common association of her name with sins of immorality. But Mary was indeed a woman who, Christ had liberated from demonic bondage. She is described as a woman "out of whom had come seven demons" (Luke 8:2) Mary was from the village of Magdala, which seemed to be a hotbed of demonic activity. None of the demonized individuals in the New Testament are explicitly associated with immoral behavior. Most of them were regarded as outcasts and pariahs by polite society. Scripture invariably presents them to us as victims with utterly ruined lives.*

*John MacArthur*

1. How does the place in which a woman grows up make her more susceptible to certain types of sin or evil influence?

2. Based on what you have learned so far, try to put a name to the seven demons that may have plagued Mary.

3. We live in a dark world where bad things happen. Your past may be tragic and you may have been a victim of the darkness. You may have suffered at the hands of a rapist or child molester; you may have even been assaulted by one of your own family members. We can't be sure what Mary's past included, but we do know that Christ delivered her from it all. How does her deliverance encourage you?

4. What do you learn about the promises of deliverance from the following verses?

   • Psalm 91:14

   • Jeremiah 1:19

   • Galatians 1:4

   • 2 Timothy 4:18

- 2 Peter 2:9

5. There is no freedom from Satan's grip apart from Christ. We must be careful in the way we choose to deal with personal times of pain, sadness, fear, and unhappiness to avoid the darkness that can so easily overtake us. The Psalms speak to the reality of these emotions in our lives.

- Psalm 38:17

- Psalm 69:1-3

- Psalm 88:6

6. Share a dark time in your life.

7. What do we learn about "darkness" from the following verses?

- Isaiah 5:20

- John 3:19

- John 12:35

- Romans 13:12

- 2 Corinthians 6:14

- Ephesians 5:11


- Ephesians 6:12


- 1 John 1:5-9


### ❧SELAH❦

*Dallas Willard comments wisely: Almost all evil deeds and intents are begun with the thought that they can be hidden by deceit. The kingdom of evil is built on lies, secrets, and darkness. It requires the absence of light to survive. Thus, for all its fearsome appearance, the kingdom of evil is structurally very weak. Turn on the light, and the cockroaches scramble to go under the refrigerator.*

8.  Write out the truth of 1 Corinthians 4:5. Why is it dangerous for a believer to try to hide their sin?


9.  Darkness can be seen in a believer's life in the form of a stronghold. A stronghold is a demonic fortress of thoughts housing evil spirits that:

    - Control, dictate, and influence your attitudes and behavior
    - Oppress and discourage you
    - Filter and color how you view or react to situations, circumstances, or people

    **Ephesians 4:27 is the best remedy for strongholds. What is it?**


10. Give some examples of ways we may give place to the devil.

# Mary Magdalene's Victory

*Mary always tried to be beside Jesus. The consciousness of her weakness made her long for His presence as a security. She never graduated from the simplicity of understanding that Jesus had redeemed her from sin and cleansed her from guilt and released her from bondage.*

1. Define the word **oppression**.

2. **Oppression** will come into the life of every believer. But how we respond to it will determine our victory over the darkness. We take our sword, the Word of God, and our shield of faith to fight off the lies of the enemy. Why is truth vital to our victory over the darkness? Use Scripture to support your answer.

3. Mary Magdalene was definitely a changed woman. Her victory came as she understood and appreciated the depth of the darkness that she had been saved from.

   **Read Hebrews 2:1-3. What does it mean to "neglect" so great our salvation?**

4. *He has delivered us from the power of darkness and conveyed us into the kingdom of the Son of His love, in whom we have redemption through His blood, the forgiveness of sins.*

   *Colossians 1:13-14*

   Share a time that Jesus delivered you from the power of darkness.

5.  Mary was afraid that if for even one moment she strayed away from Jesus, she might fall back into her former way of life. As Mary's Master and Teacher, Jesus would have taught her the truths of John 15:1-5.

    What does it mean to **_abide_** in Christ and why is it important in being victorious over the darkness?

## ❧SELAH❧

*If we would see much of Christ, let us serve him. Tell me who they are that sit oftenest under the banner of His love, and drink deepest draughts from the cup of communion, and I am sure they will be those who give most, who serve best, and who abide closest to the bleeding heart of their dear Lord.*

C. H. Spurgeon

6.  Mary understood the love that delivered her was the same love that would keep her from sin and close to Jesus. She longed to be with Him for her every breath. She did not want anything to come between the closeness she enjoyed with Him.

    **Why is it so important that we continue to grow in the knowledge and understanding of God's love while we seek to be victorious over the darkness?**

7.  Are you growing in the knowledge of God's love for you? Mary knew the depth of His love. What important truth do you learn about God's love for you in Romans 8:37-39?

## ❧SELAH❧

*Notice how Christ revealed Himself to this sorrowing one -by a word, "Mary." It needed but one word in His voice, and at once she knew Him, and her heart owned allegiance by another word, her heart was too full to say more. That one word would naturally be the most fitting for the occasion. It implies obedience. She said, "Master." There is no state of mind in which this confession of allegiance will be too cold. No, when your spirit glows most with the heavenly fire, then you will say, "I am Thy servant, Thou hast loosed my bonds." If you can say, "Master," if you feel that His will is your will, then you stand in a happy, holy place. He must have said, "Mary," or else you could not have said, "Rabboni." See, then, from all this, how Christ honors those who honor Him, how love draws our Beloved, how it needs but one word of His to turn our weeping to rejoicing, how His presence makes the heart's sunshine.*

C.H. Spurgeon

8. When Jesus calls your name, is there anything preventing you from lovingly responding, **Master**? Why or why not?

9. Jesus said. "If you love Me, keep My commandments." Mary reckoned the old woman dead. She was free with no desire to return to the darkness of her old life. She moved into a life of obedience, walking forever in the light with her Master and Teacher.

    **What does 1 John 1:7 teach us about walking in the light?**

**&~SELAH~&**

*Mary Magdalene never forgot that Jesus saved her and rescued her from evil. She joined up to expand the Kingdom of God. Her past didn't matter, because she was delivered from demons. She didn't need to hide it; she needed to talk about it. If God could release Mary from her bondage, He can deliver you from yours. Jesus saved her. Jesus delivered her. Jesus cleansed her. And then she joined ranks. She didn't just get a fire insurance policy for heaven; she gave her life to Kingdom building. She didn't want to use God to make her wealthy; she used her wealth for God's Kingdom expansion.*

10. Many who were on Christ's side did not take up Christ's cross; but Mary did. She had provided for Christ's ministry out of her own limited resources. Are you giving your life to Kingdom building? Why or why not?

11. **What have you learned from Mary Magdalene, her story, her struggle and her victory over the darkness?**

But Peter put them all out, and knelt down and prayed.
And turning to the body he said, "Tabitha, arise."
And she opened her eyes, and when she saw Peter she sat up.

Acts 9:40

# *Tabitha*

## Victorious Over Death

*The Resurrection is the ground of our assurance, it is the basis for all our future hopes, and it is the source of power in our daily lives here and now. It gives us courage in the midst of persecution, comfort in the midst of trials, and hope in the midst of this world's darkness.*

*John MacArthur*

If you were asked to pinpoint a verse in the Bible that defined your victory in Christ, which verse would you choose? As we come to the end of our Victorious study, we need to know exactly what it is Jesus has won for us and we find the answer in 1 Corinthians 15:54:

*So when this corruptible has put on incorruption, and this mortal has put on immortality, then shall be brought to pass the saying that is written: **"Death is swallowed up in victory."***

The Corinthians were living any kind of life they wanted to, because though they believed Jesus rose from the dead, they did not believe the dead would rise. We set out this week to prove in the Scriptures that a proper understanding of the resurrection and a proper understanding of our own resurrection is the cure for what defeats us in the Christian life.

Are you living as if you have been resurrected from the dead? It is possible to become so obsessed with the cross that we forget about the resurrection. If Jesus only died on the cross for our sins and did not rise, our faith would be in vain. One commentator made the point that "If the cross were the only work, then we'd be forgiven corpses."

But through the resurrection, the very life of God has broken into this world to give us life that is new in character and eternal in duration. Adrian Warnock author of "Raised with Christ" provides us with valuable insight ---

*We must remember that the cross is just as empty as the tomb, and Christ is now glorified, having completed His work. The truth is, we cannot be truly cross-centered without also being empty-grave-centered! Jesus was not just our prophet and priest—He is our reigning King. At the cross we learn true humility, our hopeless sinfulness, and our need of God. At the empty tomb we fully appreciate what Christ has achieved for us and receive power to live for Him. A deeper, fuller insight into the truth of Jesus' resurrection will cause our lives to be radically transformed.*

The story of Tabitha is a powerful testimony to God's power over death. The power of the resurrection moves out into the life of the disciples and into our lives. Wherever the power of death is overcome by the power of resurrected life, we see again the power of God alive in the world.

Tabitha's story is rich with application for our lives. She is a woman who lived the abundant life in Christ and it is no surprise that when she died, those around her grieved deeply. It is no wonder that God chose her to be a part of a miracle He would work through Peter. Our journey this week with Tabitha will be life-giving and we will **discover what it means to be victorious over death.**

# Tabitha's Story

1. Read Acts 9:36-43 and record everything you learn about Tabitha or Dorcas as her name is translated in Greek.

2. Tabitha's life was fruitful. What biblical commands did she live out?

   • Galatians 6:10

   • James 1:27

3. Her good works testified of her faith. How does James 2:26 and 1 John 3:18 support this truth?

4. The Greek name, *Dorcas*, means "a female gazelle" and "emblem of beauty," as does the Aramaic name, *Tabitha*. The Bible text does not tell us if Tabitha possessed physical beauty but we know that she was beautiful in the eyes of God and in the eyes of the widows and the poor that she helped. How would 1 Timothy 2:9-10 describe her?

5. Look at the fruits of the Spirit listed in Galatians 5:22-23. What fruits of the Spirit do we see evidenced in Tabitha's life?

6. How was Tabitha ministering to the widows in Acts 9:39?

### ❧SELAH❧

*Tabitha's work of making clothes and helping the poor may sound insignificant when compared to the outstanding works of the apostles, but they were enough to gain the love of her community and enough that God saw fit to restore her life. It's our love for God and the love we share with others that makes us beautiful in God's sight. Tabitha was a good woman who was so loved by the family of believers that they prayed for a miracle and God granted it.*

7. What do you learn about God's heart for the poor and the widow?

   • Isaiah 1:17

   • Deuteronomy 15:7-8

   • Psalm 72:4

8. How can you use your gifts to reach out to the poor and the widows?

9. Tabitha lived a full life and she was loved by many, but she became sick and died. The miracle of her resurrection was known all over Joppa and many believed on the Lord. God used her death and life for the salvation of many.

   **What kind of a miracle do you need in your life right now?**

10. What about Tabitha's story encourages you the most?

# Tabitha's Struggle

*100 percent of us die, and the percentage cannot be increased.*　　　　　　*C.S. Lewis*

Peter entered the upstairs room. Tabitha's body lay washed and dressed for burial. Tabitha's Christian friends and the widows she had helped were crowded into the small room. They were all weeping and grieving over her unexpected death. The widows wore and carried the garments Tabitha had made for them. They wanted Peter to know how generous and compassionate Tabitha was. She was loved and needed.

1.  What does the Bible teach about death?

    - Romans 5:12

    - Romans 6:23

    - 1 Corinthians 15:26

    - 2 Corinthians 1:9-10

    - 2 Timothy 1:10

    - Hebrews 2:14-15

2.  Read 1 Corinthians 15:12-19. How important is it to believe that Jesus Christ rose from the dead? Does the Christian faith have any credibility apart from the risen Christ? Why or why not?

3. Read Philippians 1:21. What was it about the way Paul lived his life that proved he knew Jesus is alive?

4. In 1 Corinthians 15:32 Paul said, *"If the dead do not rise, "Let us eat and drink, for tomorrow we die!"* Why do we believe that God saved us, but refuse to believe Him for the victorious Christian life? The power to rise above lives in us, but we choose to live as forgiven corpses! It wasn't enough for Christ to die – He had to rise! Our faith rests in the risen Christ!

   **Describe some practical examples of living as if Christ is not alive.**

## ❧SELAH❧

*Imagine the joy and celebration in the room when God used Tabitha's sudden death and miraculous resurrection to demonstrate His power to raise the dead. Tabitha became a witness to the real, literal hope of the resurrection. Death had truly been conquered and vanquished.*

5. Carefully read the words of John 5:24 in the Amplified Version:

   *I assure you, most solemnly I tell you, the person whose ears are open to My words [who listens to My message] and believes and trusts in and clings to and relies on Him Who sent Me has (possesses now) eternal life. And he does not come into judgment [does not incur sentence of judgment, will not come under condemnation], but he has already passed over out of death into life.*

   John 5:24 clearly teaches us that we have already passed over out of death into life. *We possess eternal life now*. How should this truth impact the way we live?

6. Read Ephesians 1:3. The Ephesian letter speaks of life "in the heavenly places" – not in heaven, but in the experience of oneness with our Risen Lord in His victory here and now, the place of the fullness of God's blessing.

   **Are you living defeated in this world, or rising victoriously above it? Why or why not?**

7. **Read Joshua 3:14-17.** The crossing over the river Jordan into Canaan was a significant moment for the Israelites and a beautiful picture for believers. If we apply New Testament principles to this Old Testament picture we will see that the river Jordan is an illustration of death:

- *We move forward from one level of Christian life to another*
- *It is the end of the self life, the beginning of the Christ life*
- *It is the end of a life lived on the principle of effort*
- *It is the beginning of a life lived on the principle of faith and obedience*

What Jordan River do you need to cross today? The Jordan represents your obstacles; something that is between where you are and where you want to go. Consider the choices below and identify the area where you struggle.

- Dying to self


- Self effort


- Faith and Obedience


8. What do you discover in Hebrews 3:17-19 kept the Israelites out of the Promised Land?




9. Consider your life without faith.

- Where there is **no** faith - there is no power
- Where there is **no** faith - there is no joy
- Where there is **no** faith - there is no intimacy with God
- Where there is **no** faith - there are no supernatural miracles
- Where there is **no** faith - there is no reward
- Where there is **no** faith - there is hollow religious activity, moralistic rules, and dead orthodoxy

**In what areas of your life are you lacking faith in God?**

&SELAH&

*In the third and fourth chapters of Hebrews we find that the land of Canaan is a picture of the spiritual rest and victory which may be enjoyed here on earth by every believer, it is a rest of faith in our Lord Jesus Christ.*

*The analogy between the land of Canaan and the victorious Christian life is the portion of every believer in Jesus Christ. Canaan was the goal to which God was leading His people. Deliverance from Egypt was only in preparation for the enjoyment of Canaan. The Passover, the shedding of the blood, the crossing of the Red Sea, the destruction of Pharaoh's hosts, would have been useless unless they led to the place of rest in Canaan. It was only by possession of the land of Canaan that the promise of God to Abraham could be fulfilled. If we were to be honest we see a vast number of Christians come far short of Canaan, being content with a wilderness experience. Oh they are saved but not enjoying the possession of all their inheritance in Christ.*

10. It is possible that the Israelites became comfortable in the wilderness. After all, the manna wasn't really that bad and it beat being slaves in Egypt. Are you comfortable in the wilderness? Why or why not?

11. Often our struggle to have victory over death is the faith to let our old woman ***die.*** You must bury her! Your new life in Christ is where you accept and enjoy the forgiveness of sin and no longer allow guilt or your past failures to stifle your walk. Cement the following truths of these Scriptures into your heart and mind:

    • Romans 8:1

    • 2 Corinthians 5:17

    • Hebrews 9:14

# Tabitha's Victory

*Everything that "death" means to us, the end of life, the totality of decay, the ultimate defeat, the ultimate separation, the ultimate of hopelessness, and the ultimate of powerlessness, was defeated by Christ on our behalf.*

1. It is interesting to note that in Acts 9:36 Tabitha is named as a "disciple". This is the only place in Scripture where this word is used. It is the Greek word "mathetria" which means female pupil. She was a student of the Word of God. She understood the life of a disciple.

   **How did her life reflect the reality of Galatians 2:20?**

2. Acts 9:41 reveals that when Peter brought Tabitha back to life he presented her to the saints *and* widows. Many of those in Joppa who believed on the Lord would have been the widows who Tabitha ministered to through her sewing. It is no wonder God used her death and life to bring many to salvation.

   **Write out 2 Corinthians 5:14 and 15.**

3. Every Christian's life is marked by windows of opportunity that demand that they take a radical step of faith in order to follow Christ and fulfill His agenda for their life. Tabitha was no longer living for herself but for Christ and His will for her life. She gave her life selflessly so that the poor and widowed in Joppa would come to know Christ. Little did she know, as she was faithful, that God would do exceedingly and abundantly more than she could ever think or imagine. That is the power of the resurrected life!

   **Do you believe that God wants to use your ordinary life to do extraordinary things? Explain your answer.**

*1 Timothy 6:12 exhorts us to fight the good fight of faith and lay hold on eternal life. Other translations read: take hold of, grab hold of, keep your grip on, seize. Eternal life should be our life today, a life for our present daily living. Having been called to eternal life, we now should lay hold on this life, live this life, and have our whole being according to this life.*

4.  Believers are called to walk in the reality of eternal life now! Jesus Christ is our Great High Priest who lives forever, according to the power of an endless life.

    **Write out Hebrews 7:15-17.**

5.  **Read this insight on Hebrews 7:15-17 from Andrew Murray's book, <u>The Holiest of All.</u>**

    *Through unbelief and sloth, the majority of Christians know little of the power of an endless life. Jesus Christ is a Priest "according to the power of an endless life". These precious words are the key to the higher life. Christ's Priesthood acts as an inner life within us, as our own life, so that it is our very nature to delight in God and in His will. His priesthood acts as an inner life within us, lifting us up, not in thought but in spirit and truth, into a vital fellowship with God.*

    *He breathes His own life in us, and He works it in as the power of life, a life that is strong and healthy because it is His own life from heaven. A life that never for a moment needs know a break or an interruption because it is the life of eternity, the life maintained in us by Him who is a Priest forever, a Priest who abideth continually.*

    **Describe in your own words what it means to live in the power of an endless life. Use Scripture to support your answer.**

6.  *To lay hold on eternal life* means to keep an eternal perspective. What do we learn about an eternal perspective in Colossians 3:1-4?

7.  What do we need to remember about trials in 2 Corinthians 4:16-18?

8.  Read 1 John 3:2-3. What kind of life will we be living if we are living in the hope of our resurrection?

9.  Jude 21 instructs us to keep ourselves in the love of God, looking for the mercy of our Lord Jesus Christ unto eternal life. List some practical ways we can keep ourselves in the love of God until He takes us home to be with Him.

10. It must have been amazing for Tabitha to have been brought back to life; to realize that what she believed about the power of God was true, but she would die again. When we experience our resurrection we will never die again.

    **What other exciting fact do we learn about our resurrection in 1 Corinthians 15:42-44?**

11. We have not had the reality of Tabitha's experience, but 2 Corinthians 5:1-8 teaches us that we can be confident of and assured of our resurrection. What is the believer's guarantee of resurrection and how do these verses encourage you?

12. Won't it be exciting to sit down and talk with Tabitha in heaven? What about heaven excites you the most? Use Scripture to support your answer.

13. **What have you learned from Tabitha, her story, her struggle and her victory over death**?

14. Who is your favorite victorious woman?

15. What wisdom will you glean from her life and how will you practically apply it?

*As we come to the end of our study, we celebrate with our sisters in the New Testament, as they walked victoriously with Jesus. Their stories are forever etched upon our hearts. Their struggles closely identify with ours. In all things they were more than conquerors through the God that loved them. May we closely follow their footsteps and forever be...*

Victorious

# About the Author

Margy Hill's passion and calling for women's ministry led her to start the Women's Ministry Connection where she encourages and exhorts women leaders in ministry. God has given her the opportunity to speak into the lives of women of all ages and church backgrounds.

She loves to teach and share her passion for the Word of God to stir women to a deeper and more abundant relationship with Jesus and to encourage and equip them to walk in the fullness of their callings.

Her gift for writing has led her to write several Bible studies to help women develop a desire to dig deeper into the Word of God. With challenging questions and everyday application, her studies have been widely used throughout churches in the United States.

Margy speaks and teaches for women's conferences, retreats and seminars and is also known for her "Hope for the Hurting Heart" training seminars to help equip women to counsel confidently from the Word of God.

Margy resides in Newport News, Virginia and is blessed to be able to serve with her husband who is the "Reaching Around" Pastor at Calvary Chapel Newport News. She loves being a part of the women's ministry team, serving the women in weekly Bible study.

For more information, visit her website at www.wmconnection.org.

Made in the USA
San Bernardino, CA
24 August 2015